MAOISM AND THE
CHINESE REVOLUTION
A Critical Introduction

***Revolutionary
Pocketbooks***

MAOISM AND THE CHINESE REVOLUTION
A Critical Introduction

Elliott Liu

Note: This book draws on many sources from different time periods and thus mixes Wade-Giles and Pinyin forms of transliteration. The author has done his best to standardize names and places.

Maoism and the Chinese Revolution: A Critical Introduction
Elliott Liu
This edition copyright © 2016 PM Press

ISBN: 978-1-62963-1-370
Library of Congress Control Number: 2016930959

Cover by John Yates/Stealworks
Layout by Jonathan Rowland based on work by briandesign

10 9 8 7 6 5 4 3 2 1

PM Press
PO Box 23912
Oakland, CA 94623
www.pmpress.org

Copublished with:
thoughtcrime ink
C/O Black Cat Press
4508 118 Avenue
Edmonton, Alberta T5W 1A9
www.thoughtcrimeink.com

Printed in the USA by the Employee Owners of Thomson-Shore in Dexter, Michigan. www.thomsonshore.com

*To my mother and father, and to
my partners and comrades.*

■ CONTENTS

IV. The Cultural Revolution

V. Conclusions

Further Reading

Notes

Who are our enemies? Who are our friends? This is a question of the first importance for the revolution.
—Mao Tse-tung, Analysis of the Classes in Chinese Society, 1926

■ INTRODUCTION

The Chinese Revolution was one of the great world-historical revolutions of the twentieth century. It included the overthrow of a dynastic system that had governed China for over two thousand years; a period of rapid modernization and the growth of anarchist and communist politics in East Asia; two decades of mobile rural warfare, culminating in the triumph of a state socialist project; and finally, a series of external conflicts and internal upheavals that brought the country to the brink of civil war and led to the emergence of the capitalist dreadnought that stands to shape the course of the twenty-first century. One fruit of this rich historical experience is Maoism.

The term "Maoism" is used to describe syntheses of the theory and strategy that Mao Zedong developed from the 1920s to the 1970s, alongside his allies in the Chinese Communist Party. Different political tendencies use the word to foreground different elements of Mao's thought and practice, but in its various iterations Maoism has made a great impact on the U.S. revolutionary left. In the 1960s, many groups in the black liberation, Chicano, and Puerto Rican movements, and later the New Communist movement, looked to China for inspiration. Mao's influence continues today not only in well-established groups such as the Revolutionary Communist Party and the two Freedom Road Socialist Organizations, but also through younger groupings such as the Revolutionary Student Coordinating Committee and the New Afrikan Black Panther Party–Prison Chapter. If a wave of social movement is to appear in the United States in the coming years, Maoist politics are likely to be a significant element of its revolutionary wing.

Given the persistence of Maoism, today's revolutionaries must ask: What are the central pillars of Maoist politics, in their various forms? In what historical circumstances did these elements emerge, and how were they shaped by their context? How have these ideas been interpreted and applied in revolutionary movements? How might these politics help or hinder us in developing a revolutionary movement for today? This book offers a set of preliminary answers to these questions. In the pages below, I provide a brief survey of the fifty-year Chinese revolutionary experience for militants who are unfamiliar with it, and contextualize the main elements of Maoist politics within that history. Along the way, I offer a critical analysis of the Chinese Revolution and Maoist politics from an anarchist and communist perspective.

While I disagree with him on particulars, my take on the revolution is in broad agreement with the central claims of Loren Goldner's controversial "Notes Toward a Critique of Maoism," published online in October 2012.[1] The Chinese Revolution was a remarkable popular peasant war led by Marxist-Leninists. Taking the helm of an underdeveloped country in the absence of a global revolution, the Chinese Communist Party acted as a surrogate bourgeoisie, developing the economy in a manner that could be called "state capitalist." The exploitation and accumulation around which Chinese society was subsequently organized transformed the party into a new ruling class, with interests distinct from those of the Chinese proletariat and peasantry. Mao's wing of the party tried to evade the problems of bureaucratization and authoritarianism, using the Soviet experience as blueprint and foil. But even as they called forth popular movements, Mao and his allies were continually forced to choose between sanctioning the overthrow of the system that guaranteed their class position or repressing the very popular energies they claimed to represent. Mao and his allies repeatedly chose the latter, beating back the revolutionary self-activity of the Chinese proletariat and ultimately clearing the way for openly capitalist rule after Mao's death.

My take on the various components of Maoist politics varies, depending on the philosophical, theoretical, strategic, or methodological element in question. In general, I consider Maoism to be an internal critique of Stalinism that fails to break with Stalinism. Over many years, Mao developed a critical understanding of Soviet society, and of the negative symptoms it displayed. But at the same time, he failed to locate the cause of these symptoms in the capitalist social relations of the USSR and so retained many shared assumptions with the Stalinist model in his own thinking. Thus Mao's politics remained fundamentally Stalinist in character, critiquing the USSR from a position as untenable in theory as it was eventually proven in practice. This book makes an initial attempt to interrogate Maoist concepts in this context. Other militants will have to carry the task further. Only when Maoism is subjected to an immanent critique and "digested" in this manner will it be possible to effectively re-embed elements of Maoism in a coherent political project adequate to our present situation.

To develop our account further, we must examine the broad arc of the Chinese revolutionary experience. We begin at the transition from the late nineteenth to the early twentieth century, when modern China was born in toil and bloodshed.

I.

■ PROLOGUE: THE FIRST CHINESE REVOLUTION

1. The Emergence of Modern China

Revolutionary politics emerged in China during a contradictory period of economic and political transformation. The 1800s saw China's precapitalist economy and bureaucracy shaken by rapid industrialization and conflict with the West. These circumstances entailed massive social upheaval and led to the establishment of a modern nation-state, the development of anarchist and communist movements, and eventually the emergence of Maoism.

In the mid-nineteenth century, Britain opened Chinese markets to foreign products through a series of imperialist conquests known as the Opium Wars. The technologically advanced British military delivered punishing losses to the Qing dynasty, won control of Hong Kong, and forced down trade barriers to British goods. It was a powerful blow to Chinese imperial pride, as the defeat marked the first time in centuries the Chinese state had suffered so decisive a loss to a foreign power. Other imperialist powers followed suit in later decades, forcing open Chinese markets at gunpoint, imposing war debts, and taking control of "concession" territories on the Chinese mainland where they established commercial zones. The French, Dutch, Russians, Americans, and Japanese all seized chunks of China in this manner throughout the late 1800s.

Imperialist domination generated unrest in Chinese society, even as its Qing rulers struggled to modernize the empire. The

Taiping and Boxer rebellions swept China in the 1800s, attacking both imperialist powers and the Qing state itself. With the turn of the century, an entire generation of Chinese intellectuals turned to revolution. Confucian education was abolished in 1905, and many Chinese students traveled to Tokyo, Paris, or London to study Western natural and social sciences. As peasant and worker rebellions grew, this layer of intellectuals imagined the formation of a Chinese state on par with other global powers. Popular unrest culminated in the 1911 overthrow of the Qing dynasty, and the founding of the first Chinese republic. Soon afterward, the "Revolutionary Alliance," a group of secret societies that had helped stage the revolution, formed the nationalist Kuomintang (KMT) party under the leadership of Sun Yat-Sen.

The overthrow of the Qing dynasty only deepened the social turmoil, however. By 1916 the state had collapsed into a checkerboard of territories controlled by feuding warlord armies, and imperialists continued to dominate the coastal areas. In 1919, the nationalist May Fourth Movement drew thousands into the streets to demand Chinese unity against imperialist domination. A small group of revolutionaries emerged from this upsurge to found the Communist Party of China (CCP) in 1921. The party held its first congress on a boat in a lake in Changsha, in Hunan Province, with thirteen delegates representing fewer than sixty members in total.[1] From this tiny beginning, the CCP quickly grew to a party of tens of thousands. The party centered its activity in the struggles of the growing Chinese proletariat, which itself was just one explosive fraction of the impoverished Chinese populace.

China in 1920 remained a predominantly peasant country, dependent on the work of five hundred million agricultural laborers whose living conditions were rapidly deteriorating. After the "medieval renaissance" of the Tang and Sung dynasties stalled out in the 1500s, China entered a "dynastic cycle" of booms and busts, the causes of which remain a subject of debate for economic historians. Throughout the 1800s population expanded steadily with no rise in agricultural productivity, and living standards fell. A highly unequal distribution of land strangled the peasant plot: the average family farmed a mere 3.3 acres into the 1930s.[2] Drought and famine became common occurrences, as did the practice of selling children into servitude, or marrying young women against their will to rich landowners, to stave off destitution. The collapse of the Qing state only intensified the exploitation, with landlords and warlords seizing up to half of annual harvests in rents, and local officials engaging in tax gouging or debt schemes to keep peasants in perpetual servitude. Under these pressures, the traditional peasant kinship structure began to fracture.[3] Mass peasant movements emerged that united the peasantry across clan lineages and broke traditional ties with the landlord class.[4]

China in 1920 was also being transformed by industrialization. As industry grew in coastal cities such as Shanghai, the proletariat expanded at a heady rate. There were a million workers in China in 1919, and the number doubled by 1922. While small relative to the population, the Chinese working class was highly militant and well connected to the workers' movement at its world-historic height. In 1922 there were 91 strikes across the country involving 150,000 workers. In 1924, 100,000 workers marched in Shanghai to celebrate May Day, demanding an eight-hour day at a time when local workdays stretched from 12 to 16 hours. In 1925, 400,000 workers from Beijing to Guangzhou launched strikes and demonstrations against foreign exploitation.[5] The CCP thrived in this class struggle, and grew in size.

Perched atop the massive peasantry and restive proletariat were a bloated landlord class and a stillborn capitalist bourgeoisie. Some bourgeois layers developed in the niches of the international trade imposed by foreign powers, and were thus sympathetic to imperialist forces. Others emerged in sectors that were threatened by outside imports, or otherwise hampered by the imperialist presence, and these tended to sympathize with nationalist sentiment. Many members of the bourgeoisie had themselves only recently emerged from the wealthy peasantry, and so used their profits to purchase land in the countryside. This strategy not only stunted industrial development but also further concentrated land ownership in a few privileged hands, and intensified rural exploitation according to the demands of capital accumulation.

With this configuration of class forces, China displayed all the explosive potentials and glaring contrasts of a semi-colonial nation in the 1920s: It boasted a vast agricultural economy, much of it operating outside capitalist relations of production, yet increasingly exploited by its integration in global flows of capital. It was ruled by a stagnant landlord class and a weak, foreign-dominated bourgeoisie, which were disinclined to carry out a thoroughgoing bourgeois revolution and transform the national economy. And it possessed a numerically small working class that nonetheless displayed all the militancy and revolutionary consciousness of the contemporary global workers' movement. How would these different classes relate to each other in a revolutionary movement? What role should communist forces play in the development of such a revolution? These questions became central to the CCP throughout the 1920s. Every step of the way, the party was guided organizationally and politically by the recently founded USSR through the Third International, or Comintern.

2. The Comintern: State Capitalist Foreign Policy

After the Russian Revolution of 1917, the Soviet Union held undisputed leadership over the world communist movement. This was true too in China, where the CCP developed under the close direction of the Comintern. The CCP was profoundly shaped by this relationship, both modeling itself after the Stalinist interpretation of Leninism, and working to break from Soviet control. This tension would become a defining feature of Maoism.

The history of the USSR and the Comintern is too lengthy to detail here, but some brief comments are necessary to frame its role in the Chinese Revolution. The Comintern was established in 1919 in Moscow, to direct what was seen at the time as an impending world revolution. The Russian Revolution had opened the floodgates, and now, it was believed, revolution would sweep the Western powers in quick succession, followed by the rest of the globe. But these hopes were dashed as the wave of working-class revolt after World War I met defeat—notably in the failed German insurrections of 1918–19, and the defeated Italian factory occupations of 1920. These developments caught Russian revolutionaries by surprise. For decades, Russian socialists believed their revolution would occur in tandem with a wave of upheavals in the developed capitalist countries, culminating in a world transition to socialism. Now they found themselves trapped in an undeveloped nation, surrounded by hostile powers, with little chance of world revolution breaking out anytime soon.

In this climate, the Soviet state went on the defensive. The turn was most clearly expressed in 1921, when the party suppressed the Kronstadt uprising, and established the New Economic Policy.[6] After Lenin's death in 1924, a theory of "socialism in one country" was developed by Joseph Stalin and Nikolai Bukharin (who would eventually be tried and executed by Stalin in 1938). The theory claimed it was possible to fundamentally break with capitalist social relations, and establish a socialist society, within the institutional framework of a single nation-state. The Soviet state thus came to be viewed as an "outpost" of socialism in a capitalist world, whose survival alone sustained the possibility of world revolution in a reactionary period.

Stalin's theory distorted Marx's understanding of revolution and the material basis for socialism. Yet the Russian party was compelled to reform its theory in part out of material necessity. Finding themselves in control of an underdeveloped country, the rulers of would-be communist Russia chose to act as a surrogate bourgeoisie, in place of the ruling classes they had just deposed. After nationalizing industry and sanctioning the return of market relations in the countryside to address food shortages, the party carried out "primitive socialist accumulation" in the 1930s, hyper-exploiting the peasantry to feed the cities and fund the state, and thereby sustain a program of rapid industrial development. Russian leaders believed they could carry out these tasks while remaining revolutionary communists; they were wrong.[7]

As Marx argued, social being ultimately determines social consciousness. Though the Soviet and Comintern leaders may have thought they were defending world revolution, they were increasingly simply defending the foreign policy interests of an emerging state capitalist ruling class, which represented the world proletariat in name only. The theoretical orthodoxy produced in the USSR, and disseminated globally through the Comintern until World War II, was profoundly marked by this experience. What we today call "Stalinism" is essentially a distorted version of Marxist theory, taken up and reworked in the service of capital. In addition to the doctrine of socialism in one country, its building blocks include the substitution of the vanguard party for the self-activity of the proletariat, a conception of revolutionary transition separated into rigid stages, and a reductive materialist theory of knowledge and practice, which will be explored further below. This was the body of ideas upon which Chinese revolutionaries based their conception of revolution and developed their own theory in turn.

When the CCP emerged in China in the 1920s, the Comintern was in its so-called "Second Period" under the leadership of Grigory Zinoviev (who would be tried and executed by Stalin in 1936). In this period, the Comintern rejected the possibility of world revolution in the near-term and prioritized defending the Soviet state from the imperialist encroachment. The Comintern thus actively supported nationalist movements in territories controlled by the imperialist powers. It also imposed the Bolshevik vanguard party as the universal model for communist parties across the globe and demanded the strict subordination of parties in other countries to the demands of the Comintern in Moscow. Comintern members believed this approach would further the world revolution—an aim they considered synonymous with the defense of the Soviet state—but it objectively had the opposite effect.

3. The Disaster of 1927

Throughout the 1920s the Comintern dispatched advisors and funds to the CCP in China. In 1923, Comintern advisor Mikhail Borodin instructed the CCP to cease building an independent party, and merge its organization with the nationalist KMT. In line with the geopolitics of the Soviet state, and its interpretation of Lenin's *Imperialism: The Highest Stage of Capitalism*, Borodin believed a united nationalist movement in China would weaken global capitalism and thereby defend the USSR.[8] The party followed the Comintern's directives and fused with the

KMT in 1924, over the objections of some of its cadre. The same year, the Comintern helped establish the Whompoa Military Academy in Guangzhou, to help train the KMT military. Sun Yat-Sen died the following year, and KMT leadership was taken over by Chiang Kai-Shek. In 1926, Chiang was accepted as an honorary member of the Comintern, and the KMT was incorporated as an associate party.

Popular rebellion continued to grow in the cities and the countryside. The "May Thirtieth Movement" erupted in 1925, after protesters were killed in Shanghai's imperialist districts, leading to strikes across China's industrial areas. A wave of peasant insurrections swept Hunan Province in the following months. As the party participated in both of these struggles, it ballooned in size. From only 1,000 members at the start 1925, membership leapt to 10,000 with the May Thirtieth Movement; 30,000 by July 1926; and 58,000 by April 1927. The KMT was also emboldened by the wave of rebellions. In 1926, Chiang Kai-Shek launched a military campaign to unify China and bring warlordism to an end: the Northern Expedition. CCP cadres worked in tandem to help bring the KMT to power. As Chiang's armies moved through southern China, the party mobilized 1.2 million workers and 800,000 peasants in a series of strikes and uprisings.[9]

Yet as the KMT ascended, its antagonism with the CCP became ever more apparent. After being brought to power in Guangzhou by a general strike, Chiang disbanded the leading Canton–Hong Kong strike committee and imprisoned party cadres. At this "betrayal" many CCP members moved to split with the KMT but were prevented from doing so by Borodin, who instructed CCP members to apologize to Chiang and refrain from conducting agrarian reforms or seizing private property in the province. The party's leaders dutifully followed suit.

With working-class militancy stifled in the south, Chiang launched his military expedition in June 1926. Again the CCP organized strikes and uprisings ahead of Chiang's advancing army, and by February 1927, KMT troops were approaching the working-class stronghold of Shanghai. The Shanghai General Labor Union called for a general strike to usher Chiang to power, fielding 350,000 workers in street battles, but Chiang halted his forces at the outskirts of the city and waited for the movement to exhaust itself. Only after a second wave of street fighting brought 500,000–800,000 workers into the streets, at great human cost, did Chiang take the city. With the industrial heart of China under his control and the workers exhausted, Chiang ordered his First Division troops—composed of revolutionary soldiers from Shanghai—out of the area. He then executed a purge of all communist forces in the city. CCP members were rounded up in raids on union and party offices. Hundreds were imprisoned, and others were executed in the street by gunshot or beheading. The Shanghai purge was repeated across KMT territory over the following year, in a mass crackdown that killed as many as 200,000 CCP members and militant workers. It was a crushing blow to the working-class movement.[10]

Chiang's "coup" didn't pass unchallenged: in Wuhan, left-wing elements of the KMT split with Chiang. The CCP leadership sought to take the lead by forming soviets in the city but was again restrained by the Comintern. To Stalin, the left-KMT government was the "center of the revolutionary movement" in China, and the CCP should actively support it, not supersede it. The party relented, thereby clearing the way for the KMT government in Wuhan to conduct *its own* suppression of the communists in May 1927, before reuniting with Chiang. At this point, Borodin and other Comintern advisors were forced to flee China.[11] By late 1927 the Comintern had run out of bourgeois allies, and it finally reversed course, calling for a split with the KMT and the immediate formation of worker and peasant soviets. It was too late: a "Canton commune" briefly flared to life in Guangzhou in December 1927, with little popular participation. It was crushed by local armies, leaving another 5,000 revolutionaries dead.[12]

The Comintern's interventions in the 1920s expressed the contradictions of would-be revolutionaries at the helm of a capitalist state. On the one hand, leaders such as Stalin, Zinoviev and Bukharin believed worker and peasant power was the goal of revolutionary movements in underdeveloped contexts, and they advocated for it in word. On the other hand, they were compelled to prioritize building strong nationalist allies, as the shortest path to undermining other world imperialist powers and thereby defending the Soviet state. This was the line they followed in deed, repeatedly constraining, limiting, and delaying class struggle, and ultimately guaranteeing its defeat. The experience fundamentally altered the path of Chinese communism.

4. The Turn to the Countryside

The debacles of 1927 decimated the working-class movement, and permanently undermined the relationship between the working class and the CCP. In 1927, three million Chinese workers were in trade unions, but by 1928 that number was halved, and by 1932 the number shrank to 410,000. Class struggles throughout the 1930s remained defensive in character, and were often dominated by corporatist unions set up under Chiang's regime. In some cases striking workers berated CCP cadres, or pleaded with them to leave, arguing that communist extremism would get them killed. Comintern representatives in Moscow were forced to admit that workers had rejected the party as a result of its strategic errors.[13] The broken relationship between the CCP and its class base was reflected in the party's membership. In early 1927, before Chiang's crackdown, the CCP had 58,000 members, of which 58 percent were industrial workers. While the party rebounded after 1928, and continued to grow throughout the 1930s as it developed its rural base, its relationship with the working class was irreparably shattered: the proportion of workers in the party soon shrank to 1 percent.[14]

In this context, the CCP turned its attention to the peasantry—a strategic shift that would eventually bring Mao to prominence. Mao Tse-tung, son of a wealthy peasant from Hunan Province, had been one of the founders of the CCP in 1921. In 1927, Mao published *Report on an Investigation of the Peasant Movement in Hunan*, chronicling a wave of peasant rebellions. His report identified the poor peasantry as a revolutionary class in underdeveloped China, and criticized the CCP's tendency to oppose peasant "excesses" in rural insurrections. After Chiang's crackdown in Shanghai in September 1927, Mao launched an uprising to take the city of Changsha but was defeated. He managed to flee into the mountainous region separating the provinces of Hunan and Kiangsi with about a thousand men.

Gradually Mao's military forces, and his prestige in the CCP, began to grow. First a column of CCP soldiers led by Chu Teh, then a rebel KMT unit led by P'eng Te-Huai, and finally two bandit gangs merged with Mao's forces. The resulting army numbered about ten thousand soldiers, one out of every five of whom carried a rifle. With this force, Mao managed to repel three expeditionary attacks over the following months, and carry out agrarian reforms that won him renown among the peasantry. Clashes to the north soon drew KMT armies into other conflicts, allowing the CCP to establish further bases in the rural areas of southern China. After a second attack on Changsha ordered by the Comintern failed in 1930, the entire CCP leadership relocated to Mao's base area in Kiangsi.[15] The period of rural guerilla war had begun.

The politics of the ensuing Chinese Revolution, and Mao's politics in particular, were profoundly shaped by the experiences of the CCP in the 1920s and 1930s. After doggedly following Soviet leadership into defeat after defeat, the party was forced to develop its own theory and strategy, drawn more clearly from Chinese conditions. Eventually Mao would develop a distinctly Chinese version of Marxism-Leninism through a critique of Stalin's Russia; but already in the 1930s, the party seemed headed in that direction. Its shift to rural base areas contrasted with the Russian experience, wherein a generation of revolutionaries had forsaken the countryside to focus exclusively on the urban working class. In Russia the Bolsheviks seized power through urban insurrections, and only formed a Red Army with the onset of the Russian Civil War. In the 1930s, by contrast, the CCP set out on a prolonged, mobile, rural war as its road to power.

The experience of rural warfare would establish a foundation of Mao's ideas. But as we will see, the theories developed by Mao and his allies were still fundamentally marked by the influence of the Soviet Union and inherited many of Stalin's theoretical and strategic assumptions.

II.

■ PEOPLE'S WAR FROM THE COUNTRYSIDE

5. The Chinese Soviet Republic and the Long March: 1931–1935
The CCP declared the founding of a "Chinese Soviet Republic" in rural Kiangsi Province in November 1931, with Mao presiding as its president. From there, the CCP eventually established fifteen base areas across southern China. Even in this period, however, the Comintern struggled to retain control over the party. In 1931 the so-called 28 Bolsheviks, a group of CCP cadres trained in Sun Yat-Sen University in Moscow, maneuvered to lessen Mao's influence take control of the party Politburo. Wang Ming, theoretical leader of the group and Mao's main rival, advocated using base areas as static defensive headquarters, from which to launch direct seizures of urban areas. Mao opposed this idea and advocated instead for gradually encircling the cities through mobile guerilla warfare. Mao repeatedly clashed with pro-Moscow leaders, and his influence in the party suffered.

The conflict within the CCP took place against the backdrop of constant KMT attacks and Japanese aggression. The KMT launched a total of five "extermination campaigns" against CCP-controlled territories from 1930 to 1935, the first four of which were defeated. KMT columns regularly charged into CCP base areas, only to be isolated and destroyed by the elusive and mobile Red Army. Mao developed a theory of modern guerilla warfare during these remarkable campaigns. Documents such as *Why Is It That Red Political Power Can Exist in China?* and *The Struggle in the Chingkiang Mountains* laid the foundation for classics such as *On Guerilla Warfare*, which would come later. In the same period, Japan seized control of northeastern China, conquering Rehe Province in a series of brief military offensives and annexations from 1931 to 1933. Now the threat of war with Japan hung over the internal conflict in China.

Despite the CCP's growing military prowess, the party was forced to abandon its base areas in southern China during the KMT's fifth and final extermination campaign. From October 1933 to October 1934, the KMT gradually tightened a noose around CCP territories, constructing fixed defenses with each advance. Unable to defeat these forces in conventional assaults, the CCP initiated an extended strategic retreat that became the stuff of legend: the Long March. The Long March took over a year to complete and consisted of a series of maneuvers stretching thousands of kilometers. The party traveled from Kiangsi to the remote areas of Yunan and Xikang before finally establishing a new base area in northwestern China centered in the city of Yenan. Several CCP columns conducted the retreat separately, engaging in daily combat with KMT forces and local warlords.

The Long March prompted the ascendance of Mao to the leadership of the party, a decisive break with Soviet control, and the gradual marginalization of the party's Soviet-oriented leaders. Over the course of the retreat, the CCP lost contact with the Comintern completely: communication was broken in August 1934, when the CCP's underground radio transmitter in Shanghai was destroyed. In January 1935, the CCP Politburo then held a meeting in Zunyi, in Kweichow Province in southwest China. The 28 Bolsheviks were criticized for their failed military strategy and officially dissolved. Several of the group's members joined Mao's wing of the party, while Wang Ming remained in Moscow. Only after winning control of the party did Mao reestablish radio contact with the Soviets, a year and a half later, in June 1936.[1]

The CCP escaped the KMT only after a great sacrifice: from ninety to one hundred thousand men at the start of the Long March, the Red Army was reduced to seven to eight thousand under Mao's command upon arrival in the north in the autumn of 1935. It grew to a total of twenty-two thousand as scattered columns arrived over the following months.[2] Soon afterward, however, continued Japanese aggression allowed the party a reprieve. For months, Chiang Kai-Shek had pursued the CCP single-mindedly, while ordering his troops to retreat in the face of Japanese annexations for fear of sparking a larger war. Yet the more territory the Japanese seized, the more Chiang's own base of support urged him to confront the imperialist threat. Demonstrations against imperialism and capitulation began to break out in eastern cities. In 1936, the Comintern pressed the CCP to form an alliance with the KMT against the Japanese, in line with its Popular Front strategy against global fascism (which, at that moment, was sacrificing the Spanish revolution to bourgeois stability in Europe). Mao supported the idea and opened negotiations with the KMT but refused to merge his party or army with Chiang's for fear of repeating the disaster of 1927. Talks of a truce dragged on for months.

The question was eventually settled by conflicts within the KMT itself. In December 1936, two of Chiang's own generals kidnapped Chiang in Xi'an, demanding he cease attacks on the CCP and face the imperialist enemy. Chiang relented, and a shaky "Second United Front" between the two parties was secured. Japan launched an all-out invasion of China seven months later in July 1937. For the time being, the CCP and KMT paused hostilities to confront the Japanese empire.

6. The Yenan heritage: 1935–1945

The city of Yenan in Shaanxi Province served as the central headquarters of the CCP throughout the war. Yenan was a remote and impoverished city of 40,000, where party leaders lived in dwellings built out of caves in the hilly terrain, and fraternized daily with lower cadres. From its refuge the CCP coordinated work in sixteen other base areas across China and steadily expanded its organization. The party published theoretical journals and daily newspapers, built radio stations, installed telephone lines, and founded primary schools for the populace and party academies for cadres.[3] Mao developed his distinctive theoretical and strategic formulations in this period, and the party established a common set of work methods under his leadership. Described in idyllic terms in many accounts, the Yenan period is often viewed as the "heroic phase" of the Chinese Revolution.

The party and army grew by incredible proportions over a few short years: from 20,000 members in 1936, the CCP expanded to 40,000 in 1937, leapt to 200,000 in 1938, and reached 800,000 in 1940. The Red Army withdrew from major engagements for its first few years in the north, and it expanded from 22,000 survivors to 180,000 soldiers in 1938, and 500,000 in 1940.[4] At the same time, mass organizations of youth, women, poor peasants, and other social groups were established in the villages to create alternate bases of leadership from the local landlords. In the base area surrounding Yenan, there were 45,000 members in the party's labor association, 168,000 in its youth association, and 173,800 in its women's federation.[5] Most of those who joined the party in the 1930s and 1940s were young men from poor peasant households. They were politically undeveloped and sometimes illiterate, but fiercely devoted to improving the plight of Chinese peasants and defeating imperial domination.

The CCP's campaigns dramatically transformed social relations in the countryside. Land reforms, elections, and public tribunals against abusive landlords and other exploiters became a distinguishing feature of the CCP base areas, unseating the entrenched power of the landlord class.[6] These mobilizations employed a repertoire of practices that were to become commonplace in Chinese politics, including mass criticism sessions, public confessions with occasional beatings, and the use of dunce caps or placards to identify targets of critique. Hundreds of thousands of peasants made use of the party's organizational vehicles to denounce and punish their exploiters. Landlords and creditors were punished, and new local governments were elected. At the same time, the party worked to protect the property of "the middle bourgeoisie [and] the enlightened gentry" that supported war with Japan.[7] By 1944, 50–75 percent of the peasants in CCP-controlled territories had taken part in some kind of moderate land reform.[8]

CCP leaders also established a set of standard work methods to implement throughout the party's massive organizational apparatus. The most distinctive such innovation was the "mass line," a technique employed by party cadres in mass organizations, which had first developed in CCP base areas in the south. Using the mass line, cadres were to

> take the ideas of the masses (scattered and unsystematic ideas) and concentrate them (through study turn them into concentrated and systematic ideas), then go to the masses and propagate and explain these ideas until the masses embrace them as their own, hold fast to them and translate them into action, and test the correctness of these ideas in such action.[9]

This exchange "from the masses, to the masses" was to be repeated continually, leading to ever more correct and effective policies. In practice, cadres used mass line techniques for a variety of ends: to resolve local disputes, investigate local conditions and concerns, or solicit adjustments to party policies as they were enacted.

Today many groups consider the mass line a distinctive feature of Maoism, and argue it distinguishes the Maoist tradition from Stalinist authoritarianism. Yet Mao's writings leave unspecified what kinds of ideas cadres are to extract from the masses, how they are to judge ideas "correct," how cadres are to rework and "concentrate" ideas in combination with their own, and through what decision-making mechanisms the masses should "embrace" the results. Thus the concept admits a wide range of interpretations, some democratic and others coercive. For many contemporary groups, mass line practice simply entails identifying local problems to which the party offers overarching solutions, or polling local sentiment in order to craft slogans. The mass line is rarely used to investigate everyday self-activity but more often serves as a feedback mechanism for existing political lines. In this way, the concept can easily slip into a populist method of manufacturing consent.[10]

Despite these shortcomings, the mass line and other work methods allowed the party to establish organizational roots in the Chinese peasantry throughout the 1930s and 1940s. Gender relations, however, remained a sticking point. Like most parties in the communist tradition, the CCP maintained control over the political line of its mass organizations and constrained their actions according to the party's overall strategy. With the shift from city to countryside, the CCP leadership limited the party's action on women's issues, appeased the party's predominantly male recruitment pool, and accommodated traditional family norms.

In CCP base areas land was redistributed by family unit and thus placed into the hands of male heads of households. Single women almost never received land, aside from widows. Within this patriarchal structure, women were encouraged to fulfill domestic roles and contribute to the war effort through household textile production, and discouraged from raising independent demands. In a 1942 speech, P'eng Te-Huai (then deputy commander of the Eighth Route Army) argued that feminist slogans should only be raised if they didn't conflict with other spheres of the peasant movement, and that slogans such as "freedom of marriage" should not be raised until the peasants were more fully mobilized. In other cases, slogans such as "equality between men and women" could be raised in word but not implemented in deed.[11]

An opposition current criticized this approach. Most visible was Ting Ling, a party member who had been active in feminist and free love circles in the cities in the 1930s. In a 1942 article for International Women's Day in Yenan's *Liberation Daily*, Ting argued that party policy and the culture of Yenan held women to a double standard. On the one hand, they were expected to participate fully in political life and were criticized if they fell short; on the other, they were expected to fulfill traditional women's roles and were criticized if they broke with gender norms. Against party leaders "who make fine speeches . . . about the need to first acquire political power" before addressing gender inequality, Ting argued that "if women want equality, they must first strengthen themselves."[12] Mao and other party leaders rebuked Ting's article. Ting soon underwent self-criticism and was removed from political duties for two years.[13] In February 1943, the CCP Central Committee reaffirmed that women's liberation would come through participation in production rather than autonomous women's demands. By 1944 around 60,000 women in the Yenan region were employed in weaving and 153,000 in spinning.[14]

While the CCP's approach to women's struggles would vary over time, the party generally inherited the assumptions established during the Second International and maintained in most twentieth-century communist movements. In this view, women's participation in wage labor would undermine economic dependence on men, thereby overturning patriarchal relations in private and public life. Socialist and communist parties thus aimed to turn women into waged workers before and after taking state power. Yet as many autonomist Marxist feminists have highlighted, this strategy fails to attack the distinction between waged work and unwaged reproductive labor, forcing a "double burden" on working women while guaranteeing that their labor power will appear of lower value on the market. Far from liberating women, this strategy ultimately reinforces the division of labor that reproduces gender categories, while incorporating women into capitalism as a reserve labor force.[15] In China, the CCP applied this strategy by encouraging women's waged labor while maintaining patriarchal families and suppressing autonomous demands that might upset production.[16] As a result, women's membership in the party remained extremely low for decades, hovering around 10 percent into the mid-1960s.[17]

7. The United Front

The concepts of the united front and the New Democratic revolution became central concepts for the CCP, and continue to be so for contemporary Maoist groups. The term "united front" itself has a long history in the communist tradition, starting with the Russian revolution and continuing through most strands of Leninism and Trotskyism. A united front is a tactic whereby a revolutionary party forms an alliance with reformist organizations in order to connect with their base and, by waging common struggles with them, gain credibility, influence, and leadership in the movement. The tactic was defined and popularized by the Comintern in 1921 as a way for communist parties to adjust to the global decline of the revolutionary movement and the retreat of many European workers into reformism.[18] It was further tweaked in the late 1930s, when the USSR courted relations with Western capitalist governments against the rise of Nazi Germany. Now the Comintern expanded the notion of the united front to include alliances with bourgeois parties, in addition to social democratic ones, in a "Popular Front" against fascism.

Mao crafted his own version of the united front in the late 1930s, as the CCP navigated its relationship to the KMT. In line with Stalin's Popular Front strategy, Mao argued that an alliance was necessary not only between workers and peasants but also with progressive sections of the bourgeoisie, in order to guarantee China's national liberation from Japan. In contrast to some applications of the Popular Front (and drawing lessons from 1927), Mao insisted the party retain its organizational and territorial independence. He refused KMT demands to reduce the numbers of the Red Army, admit KMT deputies into Red Army ranks, or submit the Red Army to a general command.[19] Given these conditions, Mao was willing to accept the costs of an alliance. Yet to keep the KMT and other bourgeois forces committed to the nationalist struggle, the CCP would still have to ingratiate itself to the KMT's class base. This required limiting class struggle in CCP base areas and protecting the interests of the nationalist bourgeoisie. In the process, the party positioned itself as a proto-state power, separate from the proletariat, and mediating its interests with those of its exploiters.

In *The Question of Independence and Initiative within the United Front*, published in November 1938, Mao proposes that all classes in CCP-controlled territories must make "mutual concessions" in the interest of fighting the Japanese. For the time being, the party must "subordinate the class struggle to the present national struggle against Japan." Factory workers may "demand better conditions from the owners," but they must also "work hard in the interests of resistance." While "landlords should reduce rent and interest . . . at the same time the peasants should pay rent and interest." *Current Problems of Tactics in the Anti-Japanese United Front*, published in March 1940, further details how the party will gain the support of the national bourgeoisie, the nationalist "enlightened gentry," and regional power brokers in conflict with Chiang Kai-shek. Winning them over, Mao notes, will require the CCP to "respect their interests" while demonstrating the Red Army's military abilities. The same year, Mao also moved to integrate ruling class sectors into the base area governments, apportioning seats "one-third for Communists, one-third for non-Party left progressives, and one-third for the intermediate sections who are neither left nor right."[20]

Mass meeting in Yenan, 1937.

Within this framework, the party limited itself to a "minimum program" of land reform rather than agrarian revolution. It sanctioned the seizure of comprador property in its base areas, belonging to "traitors" who had fled the area. But it prevented poor peasants from appropriating the land of "patriotic" middle and rich peasants, industrialists, or merchants. To soften the remaining inequalities, the party implemented progressive taxes, reduced rents by around 25 percent, and capped interest at a maximum of 15 percent per year.[21] Many poor peasants in the CCP's rank and file supported land seizures but were criticized or purged as "leftists" and "Trotskyites" as the united front policy was implemented.[22] "The policy of the Party," the central committee declared, "is not to weaken capitalism and the bourgeoisie, nor to weaken the rich peasant class and their productive force, but to encourage capitalist production and ally with the bourgeoisie and encourage production by rich peasants and ally with the rich peasants."[23]

Mao's formulation of the united front improved living conditions and avoided subjugating the party to the KMT. But it did so at the cost of positioning the party as a mediating force that increasingly dominated over the proletariat and peasantry, as it had over women. While safeguarding CCP control over its army and territories, Mao agreed to subjugate class struggle in those territories to bourgeois interests, with the party acting as the latter's enforcer. He thus constrained the "independence and initiative" of the proletariat and peasantry, even as he guaranteed it to the party claiming to represent them. This orientation would continue through the end of the war. Even after clashes between the CCP and KMT intensified in 1940 and the Second United Front collapsed, the party still maintained its moderate line, in order to curry favor with the national bourgeoisie under a transitional strategy known as "New Democracy."

8. The New Democratic Revolution

If Mao believed the party could ally with bourgeois elements to gain a leading role in the war, his theory of "New Democracy" proposed to do the same thing on a national scale after winning state power. In *The Chinese Revolution and the Chinese Communist Party* and *On New Democracy*, Mao proposes a conception of revolution in semi-colonial countries that combines Stalin's earlier formulations with new distinct features. He argues that the party can carry out a revolution in alliance bourgeois classes, use those classes to develop the country economically after seizing power and peacefully expropriating them to establish a socialist society.

In *The Chinese Revolution*, Mao argues that the Chinese Revolution will unfold in a series of distinct stages. The first will only aim to defeat Japanese imperialism and overthrow Chinese feudalism, "by means of a national and democratic revolution in which the bourgeoisie sometimes takes part." This initial stage is "not against capitalism and capitalist private property" per se, and will inevitably take on a "bourgeois-democratic" character such that a "degree of capitalist development will be an inevitable result of the victory of the democratic revolution."[24] Yet Mao also argues that this "democratic revolution" will not be like the bourgeois revolutions of eras past. Under the party's leadership, the new regime will practice "democracy of . . . a new and special type, namely, New Democracy."[25]

Under New Democracy, China will be ruled by a "joint dictatorship of several anti-imperialist classes" that will suppress pro-imperialist and feudal forces. With "the proletariat and the Communist Party" as its leading element, "the republic will neither confiscate capitalist private property in general nor forbid the development of such capitalist production." Yet the party will also establish state-run industries, which "will be of a socialist character and will constitute the leading force in the whole national economy." As political hegemon and captain of industry, the party will gradually phase out the bourgeoisie, and Chinese society will transition peacefully into the next stage, socialism.

From Mao's perspective, the socialist transition is assured by three historical conditions. First, he views all anti-imperialist struggles as objectively anti-capitalist. Mao accepts the Comintern orthodoxy built upon Lenin's *Imperialism*, which argues that imperial domination is a necessary aspect of capitalism in its present stage of development, and that nationalist struggles thus weaken global capitalism and bring socialism closer. For Mao as for Stalin, every anti-imperialist struggle "inevitably becomes part of the proletarian-socialist world revolution." Second, the political leadership and material support of the USSR helps anti-imperialist struggles move in a socialist direction. "The Soviet Union," Mao argues, "has reached the period of transition from socialism to communism and is capable of leading and helping the proletariat and oppressed nations of the whole world." Third, Mao believes the influence of the "proletariat and the Communist Party" and growth in "the state sector of the economy . . . and the co-operative sector" will ensure the displacement of capitalist relations.

As we will see, Mao's assessment of the USSR, his faith in party leadership, and his embrace of nationalized industry as a means of socialist transition were all misplaced; Mao himself would be forced to grapple with these shortcomings in the late 1950s. Far from transitioning "from socialism to communism," the Soviet Union in 1940 was implementing state capitalist industrialization, premised on grinding exploitation of the working class. In this period Russian workers competed for piecework wages, while facing imprisonment for quitting a job. Stalin's purges had executed the vast majority of the Bolsheviks who had helped bring the party to power, and the Soviet prison system housed upward of two million people for alleged "counterrevolutionary" crimes. In such an era, national liberation struggles allied with the USSR did not objectively weaken global capitalism but rather strengthened its state capitalist wing (what Mao would later call "social imperialism").

At the same time, Mao's faith in the party rested on what some call "substitutionism." Like much of the Leninist tradition, Mao considered the party the "brain" of the global proletariat, which possessed scientific knowledge about the nature of class society and the objective course the revolution would have to follow. Armed with such knowledge, the party could transparently represent the proletariat's interests, in such a way that it could come to stand in for the latter, thus "substituting" party for class. Mao believed the party could lead the revolution through its inevitable stages, directing class struggle at will along the way—quelling it under the united front, subjugating it to capitalist development under New Democracy—while retaining a communist trajectory. Yet such a position must ultimately lapse into idealism. The concrete social relations in which a given party operates determine its relationship to the exploited, not merely its stated politics. Just as "progressive" CEOs are compelled to twist their egalitarian ideas in order to maintain their economic position, "communist" parties at the helm of capitalist economies can also render their own politics meaningless in practice. Regardless of whether party leaders believe themselves to be acting in the ultimate interests of the exploited, the latter will continue their daily struggle against class relations on their own terms, ultimately forcing such leaders to transform their conceptions, or else repress the very class in whose name they speak—and thus the revolution itself.

When implemented, the united front and New Democracy would help guarantee victory over Japan. But it would do so by constraining worker and peasant struggles, and replacing proletarian initiative with that of the party. Throughout the 1940s, Mao would repeatedly caution cadres against seizures of land or private property, for fear of alienating progressive sectors of the bourgeoisie.[26] After the revolution the party would cultivate a friendly environment for capitalists, while preparing to put cadres in their place. In 1953, Mao assured a group of industrialists and liberal politicians,

> Some workers are advancing too fast and won't allow the capitalists to make any profit at all. We should try to educate these workers and capitalists and help them gradually (but the sooner the better) adapt themselves to our state policy, namely, to make China's private industry and commerce mainly serve the nation's economy and the people's livelihood and partly earn profits for the capitalists and in this way embark on the path of state capitalism.[27]

Mao's embrace of Stalin's assumptions was not a simple theoretical oversight. It arose from his effort to grapple with the conditions the Chinese Revolution would face in the years ahead. As an underdeveloped country in a capitalist world system, with little industry and backward peasant agriculture, China struggled to raise living standards above subsistence levels, let alone achieve the communist ideal of "from each according to ability, to each according to need." States in this situation have few options but to trade on the world market, purchase industrial goods, and accumulate capital by exploiting their own populations. Mao recognized these challenges but believed state control would allow revolutionaries to run the economy in the long-term interests of the proletariat. Yet strategies he formulated in Yenan would ultimately provide a justification for the party to act as a surrogate bourgeoisie and generate a new capitalist ruling class in the name of socialism.

9. Mao and the Dialectic

Mao also used Yenan period to deepen his philosophical acumen. For some time, Mao had been criticized by Wang Ming of the former 28 Bolsheviks group for his shallow understanding of Marxist philosophy. In Yenan Mao was finally able to address this criticism. In the late 1930s, Mao formed a philosophy study group among the CCP leadership, meeting in his room three nights a week. From these discussions Mao produced *On Practice* and *On Contradiction*, the two main philosophical texts of Maoism, in July and August 1937. In the same time period, Mao also produced *Dialectical Materialism (Lecture Notes)*, which were used for internal party education but never published independently.[28] These texts indicate Mao's understanding of the link between thought and practice, as well as his relationship to Stalinist orthodoxy. They provide a window into the philosophy underpinning Maoist politics.

Mao's version of dialectics relied on a philosophical canon that had then recently been established in the USSR. Ten years prior, philosophical debate in the Comintern had led to the self-criticism of Georg Lukács and the ouster of Karl Korsch, Marxist philosophers who emphasized the subjective, creative aspects of human praxis in the process of dialectical change. Afterward, Soviet debates shifted toward the relationship of dialectical philosophy to natural science. A division then emerged among Soviet scholars between "dialecticians" and "mechanists": dialecticians urged scientists to use dialectical philosophy to conceptualize and discover dynamic processes in the natural world, while mechanists rejected philosophy as scholasticism, and reduced social and mental phenomena to the properties of physical matter. Stalin stifled the debate in the 1930s, imprisoning and executing many scholars, and imposed his own synthesis of the two positions in the form of "dialectical materialism" or "diamat." Diamat put forward a simplified schema of the dialectical process, and proposed that thought, social systems, and the natural world all progressed according to this general logic. The dialectic, in this sense, was an objective and universal law present in all known phenomena. Diamat would remain the official state philosophy of the USSR for decades.[29]

Stalin's state philosophy became the basis for Mao's study of dialectics, through recently translated Soviet textbooks. In Yenan, Mao drew on texts such as *A Course on Dialectical Materialism* by Shirokov and Aizenberg (to which Mao gave nearly thirteen thousand characters of notation), and *Dialectical and Historical Materialism* and *Outline of a New Philosophy* by Mitin.[30] Long sections of Mao's *Dialectical Materialism (Lecture Notes)* are made up of verbatim, or slightly altered, transcriptions of these Soviet texts. The manuals served as the baseline through which Mao synthesized his reading of other first-generation Chinese Marxists such as Li Da and Ai Siqi, and of the Marxist texts that had been translated into Chinese years before: Engels' *Anti-Durhing* and *Dialectics of Nature*, Lenin's *Materialism and Empirio-Criticism* and brief selections from his *Philosophical Notebooks*, Marx's *Capital* vol. 1 and *Poverty of Philosophy*, and Stalin's *On the Problems of Leninism*. The resulting synthesis displays three defining characteristics.

The first is a form of reductive materialism that minimizes social consciousness. In contrast with Marxists who view consciousness as an active and creative process shaped by social relationships, Mao's philosophy reduces thought to physical matter itself, through a "reflection theory" of consciousness. In his *Lecture Notes*, Mao insists his philosophy differs from "pre-Marxist materialism (mechanistic materialism)," which he argues "did not emphasize the dynamic role of thought in knowledge, attributing it only with a passive role, and perceiving it as a mirror which reflected nature."[31] But just a few pages later, Mao takes up precisely this formulation: "So-called consciousness . . . is only a form of matter in movement. It is a particular property of the material brain of humankind. It allows material processes external to consciousness to be reflected in consciousness."[32] "Impressions and concepts," he argues, are "the reflection of objective things, a photographic image and sample copy of them."[33] In Mao's view, what we experience as consciousness is ultimately a property of our individual brain matter, and concepts themselves are only a kind of imprint of the world upon the matter of our brains. Later in his *Lecture Notes*, Mao carries this logic to its conclusion, arguing that Hegel's idealist dialectic was simply a mirror image of the dialectical dynamic that exists in all physical matter, much like a law of physics.

Mao's formulation reworks ideas from Engel's *Dialectics of Nature* and Lenin's *Materialism and Empirio-Criticism*, both of which were reified in Stalin's orthodoxy. In these works too, thought is not viewed as an active social medium but as a passive epiphenomenon upon which other matter leaves an imprint. Like Lenin and Stalin before him, Mao insists his view is different from the "mechanical materialism" of bourgeois science. But ultimately, he embraces a variant of this perspective. To council communist Anton Pannekoek, this variety of materialism was typical of revolutionary movements battling feudal regimes, which tended to draw upon the empiricism and positivism of bourgeois science in order to attack the ruling idealist ideologies.[34] But the cost of this perspective is that human consciousness loses its inherently social character, and its creative capacity to interpret and transform the world. Instead it appears a passive reflection of matter, which may then be manipulated by specialists who comprehend the latter's objective laws.

A second feature of Mao's writings is his belief that mental categories change through empirical observation and testing, rather than through internal contradictions within categories themselves, which are brought to the fore through practical engagement with the world. This tendency is best illustrated by contrasting Mao's account of cognition with that of other Marxists. In *Notes on Dialectics*,[35] C.L.R. James takes up Hegel's philosophy to distinguish between three levels of cognition: First, basic sensory perception. Second, "Knowledge," which organizes sense data into mental categories (for example, our experience of the color green, the texture of rough bark, and the sound of wind in leaves, all become "tree"). Knowledge categories are essential for our daily activity, but they can also prevent us from adequately grasping continual changes in the phenomena they describe. A further transformation must therefore take place: Knowledge categories must blossom with internal dialectical oppositions, and yield new categories through a series of negations. Hegel refers to this third level of cognition as "Reason." For James, dialectical Reason allows revolutionaries to continually transform their categories in a manner adequate to social reality, as the latter is continually reshaped through social practice.

In contrast to this view, Mao makes no distinction between what Hegel would call "Knowledge" and "Reason." The first level of cognition is apparent in *On Practice*: "In the process of practice, man at first sees only the phenomenal side, the separate aspects, the external relations of things. . . . This is called the perceptual stage of cognition, namely, the stage of sense perceptions and impressions." Then, Mao explains,

> As social practice continues, things that give rise to man's sense perceptions and impressions in the course of his practice are repeated many times; then a sudden change (leap) takes place in the brain in the process of cognition, and concepts are formed. Concepts are no longer the phenomena, the separate aspects and the external relations of things; they grasp the essence, the totality and the internal relations of things.

In this passage, Mao essentially says one can grasp the essence of changing phenomena by steadily stacking empirical perceptions on top of each other, until a conceptual leap takes place by unexplained means.[36] He thus sees in thought only the gradual accumulation of empirical data, generating new categories that can then be tested in practice. At this level of sophistication, there is little to distinguish Mao's notion of cognition from simple empirical observation and induction. At the same time, he overlooks how collective social practice renders received categories contradictory, and how categories themselves may be transformed through these internal contradictions. One expression of this blind spot is Mao's tendency to critique Stalinism by layering caveats and exceptions atop it, rather than examining its internal contradictions and negating it entirely.

A third feature of Mao's philosophy is the original contribution he makes to the notion of "contradiction" itself. In *On Contradiction*, Mao establishes a distinction between "primary" and "secondary" contradictions. "There are many contradictions in the process of development of a complex thing," he argues, "and one of them is necessarily the principal contradiction whose existence and development determine or influence the existence and development of the other contradictions." Mao takes Chinese society as an example: the contradiction between Chinese nationalism and Japanese imperialism is the primary contradiction at the moment, displacing the contradiction between the CCP and the KMT and allowing for the Second United Front, but when Japan is defeated the order will change again.

Mao further distinguishes between antagonistic and non-antagonistic contradictions: "Some contradictions are characterized by open antagonism, others are not. In accordance with the concrete development of things, some contradictions which were originally non-antagonistic develop into antagonistic ones, while others which were originally antagonistic develop into non-antagonistic ones." At the same time, he downplays the idea that antagonistic contradictions lead to "negation" (a process wherein something is destroyed, even as elements of it are preserved at a higher level in a new phenomenon).[37] Instead, Mao emphasizes that the "principal" and "non-principal" sides of a contradiction switch places:

> The principal and the non-principal aspects of a contradiction transform themselves into each other and the nature of the thing changes accordingly. In a given process or at

a given stage in the development of a contradiction, A is
the principal aspect and B is the non-principal aspect; at
another stage or in another process the roles are reversed—
a change determined by the extent of the increase or
decrease in the force of each aspect in its struggle against
the other in the course of the development of a thing.

In his original contributions, Mao conceives of social
reality as a web of contradictions with varying levels of influence over one another. Each contradiction, in turn, is composed of discrete elements, which may become more or less
antagonistic over time, and may alternate as the dominant
term within an overall unity. This conception has strengths
and weaknesses. On the one hand, Mao's primary/secondary
and antagonistic/non-antagonistic distinctions provided a set
of descriptive categories to interpret the complex political relationships in Chinese society. Was the relationship between
the party and the national bourgeoisie antagonistic or non-
antagonistic under New Democracy? Was the conflict between
global imperialism and oppressed nations the primary contradiction in the world today, or the contradiction between
capitalism and socialism? Mao's concepts helped him grapple
with politico-military problems, and they attest to his skills
as a strategic thinker. In particular, the primary/secondary
distinction offers a useful schema to ground the notion of contradiction in complex systems with varying centers of power
and influence.

On the other hand, Mao's contributions downplay the
active, processual character of dialectical processes, and the
degree to which objects of analysis are transformed through
them. While Marx never explicitly elaborated his version of
dialectics, he generally conceives of contradictions as ongoing,
interactive relationships, in which opposed poles presuppose
and constitute one another in a process of self-movement. This
process may lead to a negation that radically transforms the
content of the poles and the relationship itself.[38] Mao's dialectic,
by contrast, is a formal opposition between two separate elements whose content remains constant, and which oscillate

back and forth in response to outside stimuli, in a manner similar to a toggle switch. For Martin Glaberman,[39] this interpretation lends itself to a view of contradictions as simple conflicts, which can be easily manipulated by outside forces. Mao expresses this tendency when he views the socialist state as a sovereign power, capable of managing and "resolving" contradictions in Chinese society by fiat, rather than an institution itself embroiled in contradictory class relations and constituted by them.

No philosophy can be said to lead, necessarily and directly, to a specific political line. By definition, philosophies are abstract sets of ideas, which may be interpreted in a variety of ways as they are brought to bear in practice. Depending on their formulations, however, philosophies may incline those who take them up toward some interpretations of reality and practice, and away from others. Historically the reductive materialism, empiricism, and positivism that Maoism shares with Stalin's "diamat" have led revolutionaries in negative directions. In many cases, revolutionaries employing these philosophies have come to view individual consciousness as a direct imprint of the objective laws of class society, which may be discovered and manipulated by specialists with external knowledge, while the creative thought and activity of proletarians is overlooked or rejected as "false consciousness." The result is a tendency toward manipulation and authoritarianism, seen so often in the Marxist-Leninist tradition.[40]

Revolutionaries today need not replicate the same applications of Mao's philosophy. However, they must evaluate Mao's writings in a critical manner and compare them with other conceptions, in order to arrive at a full appraisal of Maoist philosophical categories. Many currents in Marxist philosophy place consciousness and creative activity at the center of their understandings of dialectical change. Mao, by contrast, recapitulates the underlying assumptions of Stalinist orthodoxy. For him, the dialectic is a universal law inscribed in physical matter and society, independent of individual will, which may be manipulated by sovereign powers possessing scientific truth.

10. Guerilla Warfare

Mao's final theoretical innovation at Yenan focused on military strategy. In pieces such as *Basic Tactics*, *Problems of Strategy in Guerrilla War Against Japan*, and *On Protracted War*, Mao elaborated a complete military framework for the Chinese Revolution, spanning overall strategy for the war with Japan, battle doctrine, and small unit organization and tactics.[41] Many of Mao's arguments are condensed in his famous *On Guerilla Warfare*. His work fused concepts from Western military theorists such Carl von Clausewitz with those of classical Chinese military theorists such as Sun Tzu and Liu Ji. It also coincided with the growth and consolidation of the CCP's military forces, including the Eighth Route Army in the north, the New Fourth Army in the south, and guerilla base areas behind Japanese lines.

In his military works, Mao argues against factions of the party calling for negotiation with Japanese imperialism, and insists the war is winnable. Certainly, he concedes, Japan currently enjoys military superiority. But at the same time, "deficiency in her man-power and material resources" prevents Japan from fully securing the territory it conquers, while Japan's internal class tensions and growing international opposition will weaken it in the long run. By contrast, China currently suffers from a "small fighting capacity," but it also possesses a huge population, great economic potential, international support, and a vast territory that can be traded for time.[42] Therefore "the strength or superiority on either side is not absolute," and given effective strategy and tactics "the factors unfavorable to the enemy and favorable to us will both develop as the war drags on."[43] In order to give Japan's weaknesses and China's strengths time to manifest in practice, Mao argues, the war must become protracted in nature.

Mao conceives of protracted war in three stages: strategic defensive, strategic stalemate, and strategic offensive. In the first stage, Chinese forces will be forced into a series of retreats, and the Japanese military will score major victories, seizing cities and territory. Yet as the relative strength of the two sides changes, the conflict will reach a point of equilibrium, and eventually Chinese forces will be able to retake the initiative and drive out the imperialists. Mao emphasizes the strategic stalemate stage as a crucial "pivot of change" in this sequence, a moment in which individual engagements have the ability to reshape the overall trajectory of the war. "Whether China will become an independent country or sink into a colony is not determined by the retention or loss of the great cities in the first stage," he argues, "but by the degree to which the whole nation exerts itself in the second."[44]

Mao emphasizes the centrality of guerilla tactics and organization to protracted war. In order to shift the balance of forces, the Japanese must be weakened by rapid opportunistic attacks, carried out by mobile forces in their rear areas. These forces must coordinate their activities with the Red Army but can operate with a degree of autonomy and may be formed on the initiative of villagers themselves.[45] In several pieces, Mao details the tactics, arms, organizational structure guerilla units should employ, and how they should coordinate with the CCP's military command.[46] He instructs guerilla combatants to

> avoid the solid, attack the hollow; attack; withdraw; deliver
> a lightning blow, seek a lightning decision. When guerrillas
> engage a stronger enemy, they withdraw when he advances;
> harass him when he stops; strike him when he is weary;
> pursue him when he withdraws. In guerilla strategy, the
> enemy's rear, flanks, and other vulnerable spots are his vital
> points, and there he must be harassed, attacked, dispersed,
> exhausted and annihilated.[47]

After driving enemy forces from a given territory, Mao anticipates that guerilla forces will be able to establish semi-permanent base areas from which to conduct operations. Guerilla units may then merge into the conventional army, and directly confront Japanese forces in the stage of strategic offensive.[48]

Guerilla actions, for Mao, entail small dialectical inversions of the balance of forces obtaining on a larger scale. While the Red Army overall finds itself on the strategic defensive, guerillas wage offensive attacks; while Chinese forces are compelled to defend their interior lines of supply, guerillas wage "exterior-line quick-decision attacks" on the enemy's interior lines;[49] and while the Japanese military encircles Chinese territory, guerilla bases in the enemy's rear provide a kind of counter-encirclement of the Japanese as a whole. The anti-Japanese war, in turn, is just one part of a larger counter-encirclement of Axis forces by the Allies on a world scale.[50] Thus Mao conceives of the war itself as a series of relational encirclements whose balance of forces can change rapidly, analogous to the Chinese game of *weich'i*.[51] Guerilla warfare forms its linchpin.

In contrast with his philosophical work, Mao's military writings emphasize the role of consciousness and practical activity in realizing the potentials of a given set of objective conditions. Rather than a mere reflection of material forces, social consciousness is an irreducible moment in the praxis of transforming the world. "Final victory," Mao insists,

> will not take place without human endeavor. For that endeavor there must be people who, on the basis of objective reality, form ideas, arguments or opinions, and bring forward plans, directives, policies, strategies or tactics; only thus can the endeavor succeed. Ideas, etc., are subjective, while endeavors or actions are manifestations of the subjective in the objective, but both indicate the activity peculiar to human beings.[52]

While people "cannot strive for victories beyond the limit allowed by the objective conditions," Mao argues, "within that limit they can and must strive for victories through their conscious activity."[53] As his comment on the "pivot of change" during the strategic stalemate stage make clear, conscious activity can even shape whether one set of objective potentials is realized versus another.

Yet in most respects, Mao's military strategy remains grounded in the same assumptions as his other Yenan texts. Rather than a revolutionary war of the proletariat and peasantry, Mao insists "the political objective of the Anti-Japanese War is 'the ousting of Japanese imperialism and the building up of a new China of freedom and equality.'"[54] For Mao "everything must be subordinated to the interests of resistance to Japan. Therefore the interests of the class struggle must not conflict with, but be subordinated to, the interests of the War of Resistance."[55] Mass organizations in guerilla base areas should therefore include "merchants and members of the free professions" alongside workers and peasants,[56] and "the political goal must be clearly and precisely indicated . . . and their national consciousness awakened."[57] Mao recommends a KMT pamphlet entitled *System of National Organization for War* be distributed for this purpose.[58]

Furthermore, "economic policy for the guerilla base areas must be based on the principles of the Anti-Japanese National United Front, i.e. reasonable distribution of the financial burden and protection of commerce." This requires implementing "the principle of 'those who have money give money'" while "peasants, however, are required also to supply, within a certain limit, foodstuffs to the guerilla units."[59] Thus Mao's military strategy ultimately constitutes an extension of his conception of New Democracy. It aims to unite a nation made up of multiple classes, and liberate that nation from an outside invader, while retaining capitalist relations under party control in order to guarantee tax revenues and food for the military.

Much of Mao's strategic and tactical thought can be extracted from its New Democratic context and applied more broadly, but some of it remains shaped by its origins. One example is Mao's conception of political work within the army. Rather than conceiving of the army itself as a vehicle for revolutionary transformation—for example, as a force supporting the armed expropriation of land from the landlords—Mao imagines it as a tool for national liberation. The result is that, just as in bourgeois militaries, divisions may arise between the army (carrying out the party's New Democratic line) and the exploited classes (whose interests are balanced with those of their exploiters under New Democracy), or in the army itself between officers and soldiers recruited from different class backgrounds. The political work *of* the military must therefore be replaced with political work *in* the military, in order to manage these contradictions.

Thus Mao emphasizes that political agitation in army ranks "must resolutely uphold the general directive of the Anti-Japanese National United Front" and "bring about a universal and profound improvement in the relationship between officers and men and between the army and the people, to call forth fully the activeness of the whole army and the whole people to defend all our territories."[60] "Amusement rooms" and political slogans may be used to build camaraderie between lower and higher ranks.[61] Rather than allow lower-class soldiers to elect officers or debate and larger political and strategic questions (a practice Mao had denounced as "ultra-democracy" since the Kiangsi period),[62] Mao limits army democracy to tactical questions and calls for a specialized system of political cadres throughout the chain of command to promote the party line.[63] In this way the Red Army, much like the military under a bourgeois state, remains a specialized body of armed men, disconnected from political debate or decision and directed from the outside by an administrative body balancing the interests of multiple classes.

From this foundation, Mao's military writings helped to develop guerilla forces and a Red Army capable of defeating the Japanese and the KMT. But they also helped to establish the army as a neutral tool of organized violence, which could be employed in the service of any political line, including one requiring the reproduction of class relations. In later years, Mao would emphasize the flexibility of the army and its ability to take on tasks such as urban administration, political education, and productive labor.[64] But just as the CCP would limit the scope of worker democracy in the factories, proletarian democracy within the army would also be constrained, its ranks subjected to the political control of party and state.

11. Rectification and Liberation: 1942–1949

By the early 1940s, Mao and the CCP leadership in Yenan had developed new work methods, strategies, and theories: the mass line, the united front, protracted people's war, New Democracy, and a particular conception of the dialectic. At the same time, the party, army, and mass organizations had grown by huge leaps, expanding twentyfold since 1937. Now at the height of its renewal, the party suffered setbacks. In 1940 the Second United Front eroded, as clashes between the Red Army and the KMT escalated into a KMT blockade of the Yenan base area. Trade with outside areas was cut off, inflation spiraled out of control, and the party was forced to raise taxes on the peasantry.[65] Undeterred, the Red Army launched the Hundred Regiments Offensive against the Japanese in August 1940. Yet the Japanese soon counterattacked with a brutal scorched earth campaign, in which the Japanese military executed thousands, razed whole villages, and deported tens of thousands of refugees to Manchuria. The party was set on its heels: by 1942 the population under CCP control had been cut in half, and the Eighth Route Army had lost one hundred thousand troops.[66]

In the face of the crisis, the CCP initiated its first major "rectification" campaign in 1942. The rectification sought to assess and correct party errors, standardize the ideology and discipline of its members, and consolidate the sprawling organization. Cadres studied new materials on Marxism-Leninism—including, for the first time, works by Mao himself—and took part in collective self-criticism sessions to root out incorrect views and secure group discipline. The campaign repeated the style of mass criticism used during the land reforms, including public confessions. At these events, participants would be encouraged to describe their life experiences in intimate detail, and renounce past or present conduct that deviated from the party's line.

Eventually the campaign veered into a purge of cadres accused of spying for the KMT, an effort led by Mao's ally Kang Sheng. Many investigations culminated in beatings or killings, which reverberated strongly across Yenan. In oral histories of the rectification, party members described the event as a kind of conversion experience, at the end of which their devotion to the party was renewed.[67] For his part, Mao used the campaign to further criticize Soviet-oriented party leaders, and cement his wing as the dominant tendency in the CCP. Shortly after the rectification was completed, Mao rose to the chairmanship of the party. For the next fifteen years the CCP would operate without significant internal factions, and Mao would stand as its unrivaled leader and theoretical fountainhead.

In December 1941 the United States entered the Second World War, and the tide began to turn against Japan. Where the CCP and KMT had earlier been forced to "trade space for time" ahead of Japanese advances, the United States, Britain, and Australia now supported them with supply routes, military advisors, and bombing runs against Japanese-held territory and the home islands. The brunt of the fighting, and the lion's share of allied assistance, went to the KMT. Yet by the time Japan surrendered in 1945, the CCP had become a powerful force, on a far larger scale than what revolutionaries experience today. The party controlled nineteen base areas, mostly in northern China, and governed about 90 million people, the vast majority of them peasants. Party membership stood at 1.2 million, with the Red Army numbering 900,000, and the militia numbering 2.2 million.[68] War quickly broke out with the KMT, after a failed attempt by the United States to broker negotiations. In 1947, the Red Army took control of the whole of northern China in a series of offensive operations. Then, in a lightning campaign between late 1948 and 1949, it seized the whole of mainland China. The KMT collapsed over the course of the year, and masses of people sided with the CCP's forces. It was a stunning military victory.

The Red Army battles Kuomintang forces at Jinzhou, 1948.

The Red Army offered a strong contrast to the other military forces at the time. The Japanese had engaged in a "three alls" scorched earth policy (burn all, kill all, loot all), which drove masses of volunteers into the ranks of the Red Army out of sheer self-preservation. The KMT fed its conscripts starvation rations, and exercised brutal control over its troops in order to keep them from fleeing the battlefield. In one case, two hundred KMT conscripts burned to death in a train bombed by the Japanese, because KMT officers refused to unlock the doors and risk them deserting.[69] In contrast to both, the Red Army practiced Mao's "Three Rules of Discipline and Eight Points of Attention": red soldiers forced local despots to obey the law, paid peasants for the goods its troops used, refrained from abusing the population, and carried out agrarian reform if not agrarian revolution.[70] It was a remarkably humanitarian peasant army. As it won military victories, the population rallied to its side, and enemy units collapsed or defected in large numbers.

While the KMT crumbled and the Red Army swept toward the tropics, peasants across China began to seize land en masse. They appropriated lands not only from "traitors," in line with the CCP's moderate land reform policy but also from all manner of landlords. The upsurge forced the party to reassert control over mass activity again in 1948. Mao repeatedly warned against "adventurist policies": "The industrial and commercial holdings of landlords and rich peasants should in general be protected"[71] he argued, and cadres should avoid "the mistake of applying in the cities the measures used in rural areas for struggling against landlords and rich peasants."[72] Even at the height of the CCP's victory, Mao was unwilling to sanction agrarian revolution from below or worker self-management in the cities. Instead he constrained the class struggle to fit the stages he imagined the revolution would follow, anticipating that he would still need bourgeois sectors to develop the country in the future.

Upon its arrival in southern China, the CCP found itself in control of the very coastal cities from which it had been expelled after 1927. The party returned as an organization of outsiders, inexperienced in running an industrial economy or urban centers. Mao instructed the army to administer the cities in 1949 but was later forced to call upon hostile civil servants to remain in their positions, and capitalists from the "four great families" that had dominated the Chinese economy under imperialism to continue running their businesses.[73] By September 1949, the party membership had swelled to 4.5 million, of which 72 percent were poor and middle-poor peasants, 25 percent were rich peasants and members of the urban middle class, and a mere 2 percent were workers.[74]

With this organization at its helm, the People's Republic of China was officially founded in October 1949. In addition to its military prowess, the new ruling party brought with it an original body of work methods, theories, and strategies. It enjoyed a close relationship with the Chinese peasantry, in contrast with the Bolsheviks' separation from the Russian countryside. And it stood poised to enact a revolutionary strategy that, while distinct from Stalinist orthodoxy, nevertheless shared many of its fundamental assumptions, including "socialism in one country" and the aim of state capitalist development.

III.

■ THE CCP IN STATE POWER

The years after liberation were a time of steady economic development and growing division in China. Drawing on the model of the Soviet Union, the party pursued a strategy of heavy industrialization and agricultural collectivization, greatly improving the standard of living in the country. However, class divisions also appeared and deepened within Chinese society, at the very moment the USSR encountered a global crisis of legitimacy after Stalin's death. Mao responded to these crises with the Hundred Flowers campaign and the Great Leap Forward. The former mobilization solicited mass critiques of Chinese society, only to prompt panic among party leaders and a vicious anti-Rightist crackdown. The latter sought to develop the Chinese economy through a dramatic mobilization of labor but led to a humanitarian disaster and deep divisions among party leaders.

Mao's prestige suffered in the course of these events, and he was removed from some positions of power within the CCP. At the same time, the Sino-Soviet split heightened tensions between the world's two largest state socialist regimes. All these developments forced Mao to reevaluate the Soviet model in depth, and develop his own conception of socialist transition. While unwilling to consider the idea that China was a class society, Mao came to view socialism as a transitional period rent by contradictions, with class enemies present in the ranks of the party itself. The resulting formulations remain a bedrock of Maoist politics today.

12. Development and Bureaucratization: 1950–1956
In the early 1950s the USSR and China were closely linked. Almost immediately after liberation, Chinese entry into the

Korean War from 1950 to 1953 brought the two state social-ist regimes together in a military bloc against U.S. invasion. Afterward, the CCP's first Five Year Plan (FYP), from 1953 to 1957, was formulated along Soviet lines. It prioritized the con-struction of heavy industry, with Russian personnel assisting in surveying, design, construction, and training. The Soviets helped establish 156 major industrial enterprises under the first FYP alone, including seven iron and steel plants, 24 power plants, and 63 machinery plants; a total of 291 Soviet projects were initiated in the first decade of CCP rule.[1]

The FYP placed industry under party control. When a wave of worker struggles broke out in 1950 shortly after lib-eration, cadres discouraged it in order to stabilize production, with the slogans "don't smash the old structure to pieces" and "preserve original positions, salaries, and systems."[2] In May 1953, the All China Federation of Trade Unions (ACFTU) reaf-firmed that the federation's main role was to promote produc-tion, not worker demands. As the Chinese economy stabilized and production increased, Mao and his allies in the CCP then pushed for a speedy transition from New Democracy to social-ism. Industries owned by "patriotic" national capitalists were rapidly nationalized. Rather than organizing worker takeo-vers, the CCP offered capitalists dividends from the profits of their enterprises, while slowly removing them from manage-ment roles—essentially, capitalists were bought out with pen-sions, and replaced by CCP cadres. In some factories this led to dramatic bureaucratization: the Ronghua Dye Company in Shanghai leapt from 2.5 full-time staff in 1949 to 52 after nationalization.[3]

In the countryside, the party aimed at effective manage-ment of agriculture and procurement of harvests. Mao believed the best way to secure these goals was by collectivizing agri-cultural lands, and he moved to do so quickly, despite hesita-tion from the party's right wing. In 1955–56, he advocated the formation of "fully socialist" cooperatives in the countryside, in which dozens of peasant households would pool land and tools, with donors receiving partial compensation, and members would thereafter share in the cooperative's profits according to work hours. The move was a huge success. By late 1956 about 95 percent of peasant households—millions of families—were consolidated into such cooperatives.[4]

As Chinese society stabilized after decades of war, living standards rose, and feudal practices such as selling children into servitude were banned. The most sustained feminist organizing of the Maoist era took place from 1950 to 1953, when a national Marriage Law legalized divorce and outlawed compulsory marriage. A mass campaign by the All-China Women's Federation (ACWF) helped thousands of women bring domestic abuse and divorce cases to court: in Shanghai in 1950, 77 percent of the city's 13,349 divorce cases were filed by women.[5] The ACWF expanded to 83 cities the same year, the only party mass organization spanning city and countryside.[6] National infrastructure also expanded. In the 1950s, 5,000 km of rail lines and 14,000 km of roads were constructed, while the number of university graduates rose by tens of thousands, and primary school graduates rose by millions.[7] By 1957, the vast majority of China's arable land had been cooperatized, and the vast majority of its industries were in the hands of the state. To CCP leaders, these changes in the forms of property constituted the transition from New Democracy to "socialism."

But economic development also rested on grinding exploitation. Over its first decade in power, the CCP steadily raised production targets across branches of production.[8] In the countryside, peasants were awarded "work points" according to the number and kind of agricultural tasks they performed, which at the end of the year entitled them to a share of the cooperative's profits. In this way, production was incentivized through a kind of collective piecework system, even though peasants were required to sell their grain to the state at mandatory low prices. (By 1956, 42 percent of all Chinese workers were assigned piecework in some form.[9]) Women's domestic reproductive labor remained unremunerated in work points and was therefore unwaged. When women participated in waged work, they were generally assigned low-wage tasks identified with femininity or paid less than men on the assumption that they put forward less effort. "We're oppressed by work points," one woman complained, "Men each day record 10 points, 12 points; the most women get are 5 or 6."[10] Peasants were paid with a mix of money wages and in-kind grain payments at state prices, which they could then consume or sell on local free markets alongside produce from small private plots.[11]

Urban workers were paid in money wages, with different rates for different jobs according to an eight-tier system standardized in 1956.[12] In order to attract workers to sectors earmarked for capital accumulation, the party could adjust the number of wage-grades, the differences in pay between them, or the categorization of particular occupations. Top party leaders were generally paid eight to ten times the wages of the lowest pay grades. Urban industrial workers were paid better than other workers across the country and also enjoyed social benefits and welfare funds supplied by their employers.[13] Yet the 1956 wage system also abolished traditional bonuses given to workers, lowering the real wages of workers in Shanghai by an average of 400 yuan per year.[14] Real wages across China would be held stagnant for years, into the 1970s, to allow greater reinvestment in production and speed up the formation of capital.[15]

In nationalized factories, workers were regularly subjected to compulsory overtime in order to meet production quotas, and administrators often hoarded medical and welfare subsidies for themselves.[16] Representative bodies met rarely, and were often circumvented. As one trade union cadre put it: "holding a meeting of cadres will solve the problem just the same, so why do we have to hold [factory management committee] meetings? . . . Workers only know what happens in one workshop, so how can they participate in democratic management of a whole factory?"[17] The alienation between rural cadres and urban workers further strained labor relations. In 1957, one cadre in Guangzhou rebuked employees at a machine works, who requested ventilation as temperatures hit 110 degrees: "When the Red Army was on the Long March, they managed to survive by eating tree bark, and you're saying when it's a bit warm in the workshop you can't work?"[18]

Like many developing countries, China inherited a stark urban/rural divide. The vast majority of the population worked in the countryside at near subsistence levels. To provide cheap food to the cities and commodities for export, the state kept the prices of agricultural goods low and procurement quotas high, which drove many peasants to migrate to the cities in search of better conditions. Yet the nascent industrial economy proved unable to absorb the migrant population, and unemployment swelled: between 1953 and 1956, the Chinese workforce grew by 28 percent while the dependent, nonworking population grew by 70 percent.[19] To stem the flow to the cities, the CCP established a highly controlled labor market using the household registration, or *hukou*, system in 1957.

Under the *hukou* system, households could only purchase food or receive welfare benefits in the geographic area their members were assigned to work. Families lost *hukou* status if they left their jobs, and faced relocation if they migrated without permission. While urban residents enjoyed access to high wages and social benefits, rural residents were relegated to low paying, labor intensive agricultural work. The CCP thereby turned the urban/rural divide to its advantage. Throughout the Maoist era, the countryside remained an underdeveloped "internal periphery" that could be heavily exploited without fear of labor migration, and which could release and absorb surplus labor as needed. About a third of peasants saw their income and consumption stagnate or decline after collectivization, while per capita grain consumption declined overall in rural areas into the 1970s.[20]

The new economy also generated a bloated bureaucratic class. The number of state functionaries employed by the government rose from 720,000 in 1949, to 3.3 million in 1952, to 8.09 million in 1957.[21] In Shanghai, the number of workers of all kinds grew by 1.2 percent from 1949 to 1957, while government staff grew by 16 percent.[22] Though not all state employees were party members, the party dominated the state at all levels. Cadres held all major leadership positions and the majority of bureaucratic jobs, and wielded similar control within mass organizations and the army. As overseers of capital accumulation, party cadres enjoyed easier access to urban residence and higher education, and promotion based on their success at fulfilling state plans. Thus even as Chinese society stabilized and developed, its class contradictions intensified. This development model reached a breaking point later that year in China and, simultaneously, in the Soviet bloc.

13. The Crisis of De-Stalinization

In February 1956, at the Twentieth Congress of the Communist Party of the Soviet Union (CPSU), Nikita Khrushchev, general secretary after Stalin's death, delivered a "secret speech" exposing Stalin's crimes in Russia to the communist movement. While news of Stalin's show trials, executions, mass incarceration, and general authoritarianism would not surprise anarchists and anti-state communists today, Khrushchev's revelations sent shockwaves through the world socialist movement at the time. In many countries, communist parties split in two over their position on the speech and their relation to Khrushchev's Soviet Union. For Mao and his allies in the CCP, the speech prompted a reassessment of the USSR's political and economic model.

In a flurry of new political writings, Mao assessed Stalin's leadership, Soviet economic policy, and the CPSU's approach to internal dissent. In April 1956, Mao delivered a speech entitled "On the Ten Major Relationships" to the CCP Politburo. He outlined a range of conflicts at work within Chinese society, such as the urban/rural divide, the relation between Han Chinese and national minorities, the relation between party cadres and non-party members, and so on. By naming the dynamics he observed "contradictions" in a dialectical sense, Mao implicitly refuted the Soviet orthodoxy that all social contradictions had ceased to exist with state socialism. Yet by maintaining their "non-antagonistic" character, he also worked to distinguish them from similar contradictions in other developing capitalist societies and prescribed policy measures and work methods that he believed could manage these contradictions and maintain harmony. Mao thus stretched his philosophical categories in an ideological manner, both to name the problems he saw in Chinese society and simultaneously to obscure their causes.

Mao followed his analysis in May 1956 with a call at a CCP conference to "let a hundred flowers bloom, let a hundred schools of thought contend." Mao's "hundred flowers" speech was never published publicly, but the slogan of "blooming and contending" was widely taken up by party cadres. Mao called on the party to liberalize Chinese society, and offer venues for the public to critique the CCP and broader social conditions. Soon party officials began planning a new rectification campaign, modeled on the rectification the CCP had undertaken in 1942, but this time open to other political parties and all social classes. The effort, which would become known as the Hundred Flowers campaign, was scheduled for 1957. Before it could be launched, however, global events preempted the CCP's plan.

In late 1956, Khrushchev's political thaw exploded into an outright revolt against the Soviet rule in Eastern Europe. In October, the communist party in Poland refused to submit to control from the CPSU and Moscow and demanded organizational independence. Khrushchev was surprised by the move and initially sanctioned the independence of the Polish party. His misstep opened the floodgates. A few days later, mass protests broke out in Hungary against Soviet rule, and by early November the uprising had turned into a full-fledged overthrow of the Soviet-backed state. Demonstrations rocked Hungarian cities, much of the Hungarian military sided with the protests, and armed workers' councils soon began to supplant state authority.

When the Polish party sued for independence, Mao had initially supported them. On November 1 the CCP condemned the USSR's "big nation chauvinism" and advocated for the right of all countries to direct their own revolutions.[23] But by the time the statement was released, the revolt in Eastern Europe had intensified: workers seized power in Hungary and were met with military force. On November 4, the USSR sent columns of tanks into Hungary to reestablish Soviet rule. Now the CCP reversed direction and supported Soviet intervention against the revolution.[24] By mid-November the Hungarian uprising had been crushed, with thousands killed, imprisoned, and exiled.

The events of 1956 reverberated in communist movements around the world, and posed theoretical and practical problems that would shape the rest of Mao's tenure in state power. On one side, the drawbacks of the Soviet model grew ever more apparent: cults of personality, "commandism" from party cadres, a brutal prison regime, and so on. On the other side, the Hungarian "incident" indicated that allowing mass dissent risked the overthrow of state socialism by the proletariat. Could state socialist regimes cultivate political freedoms and public criticism, thereby avoiding the authoritarianism that hampered Stalin's Russia, while at the same time maintaining the stability of the state and its economy? Mao's answer to this question evolved over the ensuing years, as he developed a critique Soviet model while retaining many of its underlying Stalinist assumptions. His first attempt came in 1957.

14. The Hundred Flowers Campaign: 1956–1957

Mao weighed how best to execute the planned rectification in the wake of the Hungarian uprising. In February 1957, he delivered a speech entitled "On the Correct Handling of Contradictions Among the People" at a CCP conference. Mao used his distinction between antagonistic and non-antagonistic contradictions to analyze the conflicts at work in Chinese society. Antagonistic contradictions "between ourselves and the enemy" required the "method of dictatorship" to resolve, he insisted. But non-antagonistic contradictions "within the ranks of the people" could be acknowledged, managed, and resolved through public "criticism and self-criticism," in a manner beneficial to socialist society. While disturbances such as student and worker demonstrations were to be avoided, Mao argued, they could also be harnessed in a non-antagonistic manner, in order to fix incorrect work methods. In this way, social contradictions could be ameliorated before they became antagonistic.

Mao's argument in "On the Correct Handling of Contradictions Among the People" implied a lenient approach to internal dissent, and much of the CCP leadership disagreed with him. As a result, the text of his speech remained unpublished for months, as party leaders argued over how to carry out a public rectification campaign while avoiding a Hungarian scenario. Throughout 1957, dueling editorials in the *People's Daily* debated over what limits were to be placed on the impending tide of "blooming and contending" opinions. The Hundred Flowers campaign soon got underway in the spring of 1957, without a clear answer to this question.

The campaign began as a trickle of criticism of the party and Chinese society but soon grew into a torrent that, in some parts of the country, bordered on a mass movement. By June 1957, large numbers of people were denouncing bureaucracy, corruption, and cadre favoritism in public forums. Some decried the crackdown on counter-revolutionary elements that had followed after 1949, and mass violence during land reforms, which had cumulatively killed between one and five million people.[25] Students made use of big character posters to critique authoritarianism and censorship, notably at the "Democracy Wall" at Beijing University. While students and intellectuals were the most active layer in the Hundred Flowers movement, criticisms also emerged in the army against the professionalization of the officer corps and from workers demanding better wages and conditions. A groundswell of student protests and even industrial strikes soon emerged across the country.

Criticisms came from a range of political quarters. Some intellectuals wanted China to transition to Western-style bourgeois democracy, while members of the overthrown bourgeoisie and landlord class advocated a return to private enterprise. But other currents sought to deepen the revolution, in a manner that foreshadowed the "ultra-left" politics that would appear during the Cultural Revolution. The most renowned figure of the Hundred Flowers period, a student leader named Lin Hsiling, critiqued the Chinese state from a Marxist perspective. Lin's writings argued that "the present upper strata of China does not correspond with the property system of common ownership" because "the party and state apparatus has become a set of bureaucratic organs ruling people without democracy." She advocated "not reform but a thoroughgoing change" and quickly gained a following.[26] A 1957 *People's Daily* article criticized one of Lin's appearances at Beijing University:

> She arranged certain phenomena in the life of our society—such as the division of officials into grades for hearing reports and seeing documents and the distribution of furniture by their offices—and called them a class system, saying that it (i.e., class system) had already entered all aspects of life. . . . Moreover, quoting Engels' theory that one country cannot construct socialism and Lenin's dictum that socialism is the elimination of class, she arrived at the conclusion that present-day China and Russia are not socialist. She loudly demanded a search for "true socialism" and advocating using explosive measures to reform the present social system.[27]

While intellectuals criticized the state, workers in some areas began fighting for material gains. In Shanghai, 30,000 workers participated in labor actions at 587 enterprises, and more than 700 other enterprises experienced smaller incidents. One party publication estimated that 10,000 strikes erupted nationally over the whole Hundred Flowers period.[28] An August 1957 article in the *People's Daily* acknowledged that the ACFTU unions had come to be considered "tongues of the bureaucracy, and the tails of the administration and the 'workers control department'" by many workers.[29] Thus strikes and protests spilled outside ACFTU control, and forced trade union cadres to scramble to catch up. Worker slogans boasted, "If you don't learn from Hungary, you won't get anything" and "Let's create another Hungarian Incident."[30]

In Shanghai, most strikes occurred in recently nationalized enterprises, where workers opposed wage rationalizations that had taken away their traditional bonuses and food subsidies, while preserving those of state bureaucrats. Workers also decried the loss of control over the production process they had briefly enjoyed after 1949. Shanghai workers held sit-ins and hunger strikes, marched on cadre offices, attacked managers, and organized "united command headquarters" to coordinate their struggles. Eventually the ACFTU sided with the workers, after Liu Shaoqi, then head of the federation, argued that cadres should support the strikes in order to retain legitimacy.[31] Peasants too participated in the upsurge: in many agricultural cooperatives, peasants critiqued cadre leaders for authoritarian behavior, and for failing to consult with them before finalizing production plans with their party superiors.[32]

Party leaders were startled by the ferocity of the public criticism, and many advocated for a crackdown. In June 1957, an edited version of Mao's "On the Correct Handling of Contradictions Among the People" speech was finally released to the public. Driven by his fear of a Hungarian-style uprising against the CCP, Mao revised his document to include more limitations on public criticism. If non-antagonistic contradictions "are not handled properly, or if we relax our vigilance and lower our guard," Mao argued, "antagonism may arise," especially under the influence of counter-revolutionary elements. In Mao's view, this was what occurred in Hungary: "deceived by domestic and foreign counter-revolutionaries, a section of the people in Hungary made the mistake of resorting to violence against the people's government." To avoid this outcome, Mao added a set of criteria to his speech that placed limits on mass criticism:

1. Words and deeds should help to unite, and not divide, the people of all our nationalities.

2. They should be beneficial, and not harmful, to socialist transformation and socialist construction.

3. They should help to consolidate, and not undermine or weaken, the people's democratic dictatorship.

4. They should help to consolidate, and not undermine or weaken, democratic centralism.

5. They should help to strengthen, and not shake off or weaken, the leadership of the Communist Party.

With the publication of Mao's speech, the official limits to dissent were made clear: mass criticism and even public disturbances were acceptable, so long as they didn't threaten state power or party control over the movement. With this shift, the CCP abruptly transformed the Hundred Flowers movement into an "Anti-Rightist Campaign" and began persecuting its critics.

The ensuing Anti-Rightist movement targeted around 550,000 people with public criticisms, imprisonment, and in some cases execution. The crackdown mainly focused on intellectuals, but cadres in the CCP were also targeted. For fear of persecution, the ACWF moderated its slogans, calling on women to "diligently, thriftily build the country, diligently, thriftily manage the family."[33] Lin Hsi-ling was purged from the party youth organization, and the period of open critical forums came to a close. Only after the crackdown did Mao's wing of the party institute some reforms. In many industries, one-man management was replaced with "administrative committees" made up of managers, technicians and workers.[34] In late 1958, the party implemented a system of "two participations" (cadres participating in manual labor and workers in management) "one reform" (changes to stringent factory rules) and the "triple union" (harmony between workers, cadres, and technicians).[35]

One effect of the crackdown was that the most radical party cadres, who had supported critiques of the party from a revolutionary perspective, were suddenly branded "rightist" alongside conservative elements. Experiences like this would eventually reshape political discourse in China: terms like "revolutionary" and "conservative" gradually lost their political meaning as they failed to represent distinct class interests, and were reduced to rhetorical labels for those deemed loyal or disloyal to the party at a given moment. Yet with the threat of state violence nonetheless imbuing the terms with significance, cadres and the general population were also compelled to cast their interests and demands in this rhetorical style, until "revolutionary" language came to serve as a kind of popular ideology. This ideology would explode a decade later during the Cultural Revolution, when student and worker groups repeatedly battled over the very meaning of terms like "revolutionary" and "reactionary."

Mao's conduct in 1957 also established a pattern he would repeat on a far larger scale during the Cultural Revolution.

Seeking to ameliorate the bureaucracy and authoritarianism engendered by state capitalism, Mao called forth a movement to rectify the party. However, the movement soon began to overflow the bounds he had decided for it at the outset and developed its own definitions of China's problems. Once the ferment threatened to undermine the effectiveness of party control, Mao reversed himself and used state power to quash the very popular energies he claimed to support. Only then did he institute a limited version of the reforms for which the movement advocated. This was Mao's practical answer to the questions posed in 1956. He sought to ameliorate the worst aspects of the Soviet model, while retaining his commitment to state capitalism, party rule, and "socialism in one country." It amounted to a Stalinist critique of Stalinism.

Now Mao was pressed on several fronts. The Hundred Flowers campaign had revealed the depth of dissatisfaction in Chinese society, and officials felt pressure to improve living standards and demonstrate their legitimacy. Development, however, was being restrained by China's backward peasant agriculture. Agricultural production was needed not only to feed urban workers but also to earn money for the state through exports, in order to then purchase industrial goods. Yet the state simply could not extract grain fast enough to support rapid industrialization. Already in 1954, projected grain increases of 9 percent had peaked at 2 percent in practice, while increases of cotton—an important export commodity—were projected at 18 percent but actually fell by 11 percent.[36] Between 1952 and 1960 the urban population grew from 71.6 million to 130 million, while grain procurement stagnated or fell.[37] China's underdeveloped economy was hitting its limits. Some party leaders argued for a controlled return to rural private enterprise, but Mao proposed the opposite: a mass mobilization of China's peasant population.

15. The Great Leap Forward: 1958–1962
In essence, the CCP confronted the same challenges as Russia after 1917: how could the new state abolish feudal relations, develop industry, and raise industrial and agricultural

productivity—the historical tasks of capitalist development—while moving toward "socialism in one country"? The first Five Year Plan had successfully expanded Chinese industry. But industry itself was now constrained by the low productivity of agriculture, as well as a lack of infrastructure such as transportation, irrigation, and electricity. Mao sought to address this situation through a mass labor mobilization in the countryside. He believed this campaign would produce food surpluses (which could feed industrial workers and be exported) and labor surpluses (which could be directed to infrastructure projects). He named this effort the Great Leap Forward (GLF).

The GLF remains a controversial topic. Scholars, Maoist revolutionaries, and non-Maoist revolutionaries disagree over its costs and accomplishments, and their respective arguments often rest on limited information, as many state archives related to the GLF remain sealed. I deal with the GLF here in order to highlight two points. First, the parallels between the GLF and Soviet collectivization. Second, the authoritarian requirements and human costs of the model itself.

In the 1930s, the Soviet Union addressed its underdevelopment problems through "socialist primitive accumulation," a term coined by party economist Yevgeni Preobrazhensky (who was eventually tried and executed by Stalin in 1937). Under Preobrazhensky's scheme, peasants in the countryside were forced into collective farms, in hopes of raising agricultural output through more efficient organization and oversight. Any additional grain was used to feed the growing industrial cities, and also exported to generate state profits and finance industrialization. When the CPSU put this policy into action, it sparked intense resistance from the peasantry. Stalin responded by labeling resistors *khulaks* (rich peasants) and imprisoning and executing them en masse. Heavy agricultural procurement eventually contributed to outbreaks of famine across the Soviet breadbasket. Soviet collectivization and industrialization was thus accomplished at great human cost. By 1940, over 90 percent of peasant lands in the USSR had been collectivized, and the state had managed to expand its industrial base even though agricultural productivity continued to lag. Around ten to twelve million peasants were dead, and tens of thousands imprisoned.

The Soviet experience highlights the structural forces that constrained many twentieth-century revolutions. Without an allied revolution in any part of the capitalist core, states such as the USSR were forced to buy the goods and technologies they needed on the world market. Yet they possessed a limited range of exports to sell to global capitalists and a limited number of ways to collect state revenue domestically, and both were premised on exploitative labor relations. In this context, development could only take place by hyper-exploiting the country's laboring classes, thus accumulating corpses alongside fixed capital. State capital, no less than capital in its other forms, comes into the world "dripping from head to foot, from every pore, with blood and dirt," as Marx described.

In China Mao faced similar material constraints and pursued similar goals but hoped to accomplish them without the Soviet shortcomings. The central difference between Mao's approach and Stalin's was that the CCP was firmly embedded in the peasantry. With work methods and mass organizations rooted in the countryside since the Yenan period, the CCP enjoyed a far closer connection to the peasantry than the CPSU. Thus the CCP could mobilize the peasantry through mass campaigns led by rural cadres, rather than at gunpoint.

On the heels of the Anti-Rightist movement, Mao's wing of the party pushed for a "rash advance" to develop the country. Rural cadres were instructed to establish "people's communes" across the countryside in 1958, administrative units that were much larger than the cooperatives established in 1955–56. While cooperatives had contained an average of 164 families, the communes held 5,000 households each on average, and sometimes as many as 20,000. They covered large geographical territories and centralized many of the governmental functions of the area in a single unit, including education, healthcare, and overseeing agricultural and industrial production. The results were dramatic: by the end of 1958, 99 percent of the peasant population had been concentrated into 26,578 communes across the country.[38]

Intended to oversee accumulation, the communes gave party cadres a high degree of control over the work process and reproduction of the rural population. Communes commandeered the individual property of peasant households: seed stores, farm tools, and animals—and in some cases cooking implements and even furniture—were moved to a central location as communal property. In some cases individual plots of land were expropriated as well, thus abolishing individual subsistence farming. Sometimes houses were destroyed to make way for communal infrastructure: in Ningxiang County in Hunan, 700,000 dwellings were reduced to 450,000.[39] Large communal kitchens were established to replace the household as the main site of peasant reproduction. The commune administration then allocated commune members into different work teams, to tend fields and launch irrigation projects, steel production, or other industrial and infrastructural works.

Drawing on the Yenan heritage, the CCP at first employed mass meetings and popular slogans as primary methods of mobilization, rather than direct force. Peasant leaders sat with cadres on management bodies and held forums to discuss how best to meet production goals set by the party center. Nevertheless, the scope of mass meetings remained circumscribed by directives from above. As a Western scholar noted shortly afterward,

> mass decision-making does not mean that the workers make managerial decisions for a plant or mine or commune production team, but rather that they discuss basic management alternatives, under Party guidance. . . . The CCP expected that "when the workers felt that their demands and suggestions" on production practices "were duly considered, supported and assisted by the leaders, their feeling of being the master was strengthened."[40]

This substitution of mass mobilization for mass decision-making had been a feature of state socialism since the early days of the Soviet Union,[41] but it was perfected during the Chinese Revolution. By strengthening peasants' "feeling" of being masters, within bounds set by the party, the CCP guaranteed a degree of consent that had been impossible for Stalin in the 1930s.

At times, party control over reproduction could be used punitively. State control over the mobility and reproduction of the workforce had already been enacted through the *hukou* system and the state monopoly on grain (established in 1953). Now in the communes, party cadres directly oversaw the daily reproduction of 110 million peasant households. In some cases, peasants who criticized the GLF or failed to meet production goals were denied access to food: as one cadre from Gucheng commune in Anhui Province put it, "Holding the communal kitchen's ladle and scale in my hand, I decide who lives and who dies."[42] This mix of consent and coercion allowed the CCP to mobilize low-tech labor power at an incredible level. Peasant work teams not only raised agricultural production but also smelted steel and built dams, irrigation systems, and factories, often using crude technical implements.

Once communal kitchens had replaced the peasant household, women were moved out of their homes and assigned to work teams. Officials lauded this as a step toward women's liberation, and many young women did embrace labor mobilizations as an escape from patriarchal families and villages. At the height of the GLF, millions of women were mobilized, working an average of 250 days in 1959 as compared with 166 in 1957.[43] In some work brigades, up to 80 percent of the peasant population was assigned to nonagricultural work, with women covering all the remaining labor in the fields.[44] But the shift ultimately conformed to the pattern of Third World development, wherein women serve as a temporary reserve labor force. Unwaged reproductive labor fell heavily on older women who remained in the home, while men were not mobilized to take on reproductive tasks. In many cases, villagers resisted even this disruption of gender norms, citing the superstition that "if women go the fields, it won't rain."[45] After the GLF, the vast majority of women would be returned to work in the domestic sphere. The army was temporarily mobilized in a similar way: in 1956 the army had logged 4 million workdays, but in 1957 the number rose to 20 million, and by 1958 officials claimed 59 million workdays had been carried out.[46]

Production boomed, prompting elation from CCP leaders and initiating a vicious cycle of rising expectations and exploitation that became known as the "exaggeration wind." In 1958, rural cadres began to overestimate the yields that their mass production campaigns would produce. Each level of the CCP bureaucracy, keen to prove its enthusiasm about the campaign to its superiors, then tended to inflate statistics on their way to Beijing. With these skewed numbers, party leaders then set production goals even higher, necessitating deeper exploitation at the base. The state doubled its 1958 steel quotas from the previous year and continued to raise targets for months as Mao emphasized the importance of steel production in public statements.[47] In Yunnan Province, local officials claimed a new factory was opened every 1.05 minutes, while officials in Jingning County in Gansu Province claimed more than ten thousand factories had been built in fifteen days.[48]

More than just a bureaucratic error, the exaggeration wind must be seen as a result of state capitalist class relations. Cadres during the GLF essentially acted as overseers for capital accumulation, backed by the state's monopoly of violence. Many low-level cadres were afraid to revise production targets downward so soon after the Anti-Rightist campaign, for fear of being labeled "rightist" and purged, imprisoned or executed. At the same time, all cadres jockeyed for position in the party hierarchy. While the CCP was ultimately driven by the imperative to accumulate capital, the class mobility if its members was mediated by their political advancement within the party structure. Cadres thus competed to prove their effectiveness at accumulation not primarily through free market competition but by vying for bureaucratic renown.

At the top, Party leaders believed the Chinese economy was making a dramatic leap from semi-colonial underdevelopment to communist abundance in a short period of time. In July 1958, Liu Shaoqi boasted that China would overtake the UK's industrial capacity in two to three years.[49] In August 1958, Mao predicted China would surpass socialism and reach

communism in three to four, or possibly five to six, years.[50]
The *People's Daily* and other party publications regularly spoke
of the China making a transition to a communism, where
society would be guided by the principle "from each according to ability, to each according to need." Communes overes-
timated the national food surplus based on inflated statistics, and communal kitchens soon allowed people to eat for
free, prompting a consumption boom in late 1958. For a brief
window, peasant consumption spiked along with work hours.
But the boom couldn't last.

16. The Great Famine

As peasants began to reach their physical limits, production
began to slow, and food surpluses dwindled. A December
1958 party directive instructed cadres to curb peasant "enthusiasm" and remind people to sleep eight hours per night.[51]
Soon starvation began to appear in the provinces. Xinyang
Prefecture in Henan Province experienced some of the most
acute famine deaths, with one out of eight residents—about
a million people—eventually dying of starvation. In a hard-
hit work brigade in Qiaogou Commune in Huaibin County,
26.7 percent of members died from starvation, as compared
with only 8.8 percent of cadres.[52] In extreme cases, residents
resorted to eating tree bark and agricultural waste, or engaging
in cannibalism.[53]

In July 1959, party leaders held a work conference in
Lushan to address the growing crisis. Many officials called for
an end to the GLF, including Defense Minister P'eng Te-Huai,
who criticized Mao in an open letter. At first Mao made a brief
self-criticism before the party, but he soon doubled back and
attacked Peng and his supporters as a "clique" weakening the
state's legitimacy. Mao famously threatened to "go to the countryside to lead the peasants to overthrow the government. If
those of you in the Liberation Army won't follow me, then
I will . . . organize another Liberation Army. But I think the
Liberation Army would follow me."[54] Peng was removed, and
Lin Piao, one of Mao's close allies, was installed as head of
the military. A campaign against right deviationism was then

launched throughout the party, purging critics of the GLF, and pushing the campaign ahead even as famines deepened.

The situation was worsened by outside factors as well: in July 1959 the Yellow River flooded croplands, and in 1960 droughts affected around half of China's agricultural areas. Notably, however, the flood cycle in 1959 was less pronounced than in either 1954 or 1973, and drought conditions in 1960 were less severe than other cyclical droughts in 1955, 1963, and 1966.[55] Natural calamities contributed to famines during the GLF but were not their main cause. Similarly, the economy was impacted by the withdrawal from China in 1960 of several thousand Soviet technical advisors (discussed further below). Yet most of these advisors worked in heavy industry and the nascent nuclear weapons program, with only a handful related to agriculture.[56] More powerful than all these factors was the state's drive to accumulate.

Into 1960 state procurement of grain continued to rise even as agricultural production plummeted, and famines grew widespread. State grain supplies were directed toward the cities and exports: while grain output fell in China by 25 million tons between 1957 and 1959, exports doubled in the same period to 4.2 million tons, and sales of grain to the cities remained higher per capita than to the countryside.[57] When state grain procurement was finally forced down in 1960–61 due to the production crisis, the state nonetheless reduced grain sales to the countryside by 8 billion kilos, and more than doubled exports.[58] In March 1960, Mao lauded the communes in Guizhou Province, claiming they would "make a great leap forward in the transition from socialism to communism in the next five to ten years." Guizhou eventually suffered the most reported starvation deaths per capita of all Chinese provinces, with about 5.3 percent of its 17 million residents dying.[59]

Soon peasants began to rebel, straining CCP hegemony in the countryside. Multiple provinces reported spikes in looting and theft in 1960, particularly of grain depots and train shipments of food. In the winter of 1960–61, Liping County in Guizhou saw over four thousand lootings of state storehouses. Other peasants fled their homes: around sixty thousand refugees flooded from southwestern provinces into Hong Kong from 1960 to 1961.[60] Their base fracturing, many rural cadres were forced to disband commune organizations and send peasants back to household plots to look after their own subsistence. Finally the party chose to retreat from the GLF rather than risk mass repression of the peasantry. At a party conference in 1961, Mao made a more profound self-criticism than at Lushan. Premier Zhou En-Lai drafted "Twelve Agricultural Provisions" that encouraged peasants to cultivate private plots of land, and allowed them to establish local markets for their produce. The communal kitchens were disbanded, administration was devolved to local units, and the "people's communes" were preserved in name only.

Party leaders discuss the Great
Leap Forward, 1962.

The human cost of the GLF was enormous. Estimates range from 18 to 45 million dead, with 35 million the most likely number according to three different studies.[61] Proportional to the population, the GLF thus required roughly the same human cost as Stalin's collectivization.[62] For this price paid in corpses, the GLF accomplished a burst in agricultural and industrial production that could not be sustained. Heavy industry leapt 230 percent between 1958 and 1960, and steel output grew from 5.35 million tons in 1957 to 18 million tons in 1960.[63] But many materials produced during the leap were of low quality, and had to be scrapped afterward. The CCP's second Five Year Plan, introduced after the GLF, saw 100,000 enterprises closed, steel production drop back to 7 million tons, and labor productivity fall by 5.4 percent.[64] Agricultural production plummeted below 1952 levels and wouldn't recover until the late 1960s.[65]

The Hundred Flowers campaign and the GLF left deep wounds in Chinese society and the party. Millions resented the suffering they endured during famines and anti-rightist persecutions. Within the CCP leadership, Mao's position was shaken for the first time since Yenan. Not only had his campaign led to mass deaths and strained the party's hegemony in the countryside, but it had also failed according to developmentalist standards. Deep fissures now arose over how to address the party's failures. For the first since the 1930s, Mao's wing of the party found itself sidelined from positions of influence. In 1962, party officials who had been purged for critiquing the GLF were rehabilitated, and a party conference denounced the "cult of personality" surrounding Mao. Mao was ousted as State Chairman and replaced by Liu Shaoqi, whose "pragmatic" wing took control of the state. Yet Mao continued to search for a Chinese path to socialism while out of the public eye. He would continue to develop his ideas during the Sino-Soviet split.

17. The Sino-Soviet Split in Theory and Practice: 1960–1963

As the party retreated from the GLF, a full diplomatic break between China and the Soviet Union emerged in the international arena. The "Sino-Soviet split" was expressed geopolitically in a breakdown of political and military relations between the two nations. It was also expressed ideologically, in repeated polemics between the CCP and the CPSU.

Geopolitically, the CCP grew disenchanted with the USSR as it became clear the latter was acting out of narrow self-interest as an imperialist state. In 1957, Khrushchev established a policy of "peaceful coexistence" with the West, deepening diplomatic relations with the United States even as it supported Taiwan and Japan to counter China's regional influence. Mao initiated the Second Taiwan Strait Crisis in July 1958, shelling a set of disputed islands occupied by the KMT military; yet he refused to obtain permission from the Soviets beforehand, and was infuriated when Khrushchev failed to offer China the defense of Russia's nuclear umbrella. A similar break occurred in August 1959, when clashes broke out with the Indian military on the Tibetan border, and the Soviets maintained neutrality between Mao and Nehru. Considering Mao a liability, Khrushchev pulled Soviet industrial advisors out of China in early 1960, halting a slew of industrial projects. Finally, in 1963 the USSR signed the Limited Test Ban Treaty with the United States and Britain, opposing new entrants into the "nuclear club" just as China's own weapons program was coming on line.[66]

These developments forced Mao to reevaluate the character of the Soviet state and its relationship with world socialism. He began to refer to the USSR as a "social imperialist" state in speeches and writings, and authored a set of documents with other CCP leaders that broke with Soviet orthodoxy. The texts hammered out a new conception of the revolutionary process: socialism, Mao concluded, constitutes an extended transitional phase between capitalism and communism, the outcome of which is not assured, and in which the forces of capitalist restoration may appear within the ranks of the party itself. These positions would provide the foundation for the Cultural Revolution and become central elements of contemporary Maoism.

Already in 1957, the CCP had published *On the Historical Experience of the Dictatorship of the Proletariat* and *More on the Historical Experience of the Dictatorship of the Proletariat*, in response to Khrushchev's "secret speech." Fundamentally, the documents had affirmed "socialism in one country" as a universal model: the goal of communist movements worldwide was to forge an alliance between the working class and peasantry, seize state power through a Marxist-Leninist party, nationalize industry, and raise the productive forces while opposing imperialism. Yet the pieces also criticized Khrushchev's appeasement of the West, and the CPSU's interpretation of Marxist-Leninist doctrine, insisting that contradictions continue to exist under socialism as per Mao's "On the Ten Major Relationships" speech. They offered an alternative assessment of Stalin's legacy, criticizing Stalin's cult of personality and authoritarianism while viewing him in a positive light overall. A common formulation used by Mao in this period was that Stalin was "30 percent wrong and 70 percent right."

Mao and other CCP leaders cemented the break with the USSR in a collection of articles entitled *The Polemic on the General Line of the International Communist Movement* published in 1963. With pieces such as "On The Question of Stalin" and "On Khrushchev's Phony Communism and Its Historical Lessons for the World," the CCP reaffirmed its positive assessment of Stalin and its critiques of Khrushchev's USSR. At the same time, Mao reflected critically on the Soviet model in his own individual writings. In 1961–62, Mao compiled an extensive set of *Reading Notes on the Soviet Text 'Political Economy'* and synthesized his conclusions in several articles. Mao's *Reading Notes* include detailed critiques of Soviet economic, industrial, and agricultural policy, as well as larger strategic questions over the nature of socialist transition. They shed light on his evolving critique of the Soviet Union in the early 1960s.

In the *Reading Notes* Mao levels critiques at the USSR that appear to contradict the Stalinist model. For example, he argues against using "material incentives" such as piecework and bonuses to spur production,[67] and insists parties should instead put "politics in command," increasing production by convincing workers of a political line that requires higher productivity to achieve its goals.[68] He refuses the notion that socialism is a "fully consolidated" mode of production and instead considers it an extended transitional phase, in which communist and capitalist social relations vie for dominance.[69] Yet he still insists upon the "universal significance" of state capitalism as a developmental path.[70] Throughout his notes, Mao is concerned with the proper management of state capitalist development but leaves state capitalism itself unquestioned.

In Mao's view, nationalized property—or "ownership by the whole people"—provides the material basis to overcome capitalist social relations and transition to communism. Individual and collective property can be "changed into ownership by the whole people," and the productive forces raised, in order "to progress from distribution according to labor to distribution according to need."[71] Rather than a self-expanding form of exploitation, then, state capitalism is itself seen as the path to socialism. While Mao admits "contradictions to be resolved remain in the production relations under people's ownership," he believes these consist of conflicts among state planners.[72] "The most important question" with regard to state property "is administration," not the relations of producers to their means of production and subsistence.[73] He admits an economy organized along these lines continues to generate capitalist "value," but immediately insists this value "serves as an instrument of planning" without constituting "the main basis of planning."[74]

In contrast with Stalin, Mao recognizes the social contradictions pervading socialist society. Yet because of his commitment to state capitalist development, he locates their cause everywhere except in class relations. For example, Mao argues that social contradictions may arise due to "'vested interest groups' which have grown content with existing institutions,"[75] or "'master-of-the-house' attitudes" among party cadres, which "make the workers reluctant to observe labor discipline."[76] In other cases, the productivity of collective property may lag behind state property, and thus the two forms will come into conflict through bureaucratic competition.[77] Yet nowhere does Mao examine how everyday wage labor, bureaucratic administration of surpluses, and circulation of commodities reproduce class relations in the heart of the state sector and so give rise to these symptoms.

State property for Mao offers a path to communism, if only its impediments can be removed. As a result, he insists it is possible to resolve contradictions in socialist society without overthrowing the state. "The transition to communism certainly is not a matter of one class overthrowing another," he argues, since the proletariat already holds power through the communist party. While "contradictions are the motive forces" of change in socialist society, "criticism and self-criticism are the methods for resolving" them, not class struggle proper.[78] In this way, "new production relations and social institutions supersede old ones" even as the party retains its leading position.[79]

In his *Reading Notes* Mao lays the foundation for contemporary Maoist conceptions of socialist transition. He conceives of socialism as an extended transitional period, operating on the basis of a state capitalist economy directed by the party. He believes the transition period will involve continual conflict between capitalist relations and socialist ones, and that social contradictions will continue to appear. However, these problems can be resolved through a broad application of criticism and self-criticism in work methods and mass mobilizations, without threatening state power. This formulation would lead Mao into the crucible of the Cultural Revolution.

18. An Explosion Waiting to Happen

In the early 1960s, Mao sought the source of contradictions in every location *except* the relations of production. Not alienated labor, money, capital accumulation or the law of value were to blame, but rather sociological interest groups from former deposed classes, small-scale production at the margins of the economy, and "bad ideas" in mass culture. In this way, Mao was forced to abandon Marx's analytic focus on the social relations of production in order to maintain his Stalinist commitments. If the proletariat held power in socialist China through the CCP, Mao reasoned, then "class struggle" no longer meant a battle for political power. Instead, class struggle was expressed as a "two-line struggle" of ideas within Chinese society and the party itself.

On one side was a political line that would continue on the path to communism, expanding state production and resolving social contradictions through mass campaigns. On the other was a political line that would lead toward capitalist restoration, akin to Khrushchev's influence in the USSR. Mao was coming to believe the character of Chinese society, socialist or capitalist, would be decided by which political line held sway in state power. "If Marxist-Leninists are in control," Mao concluded in his *Reading Notes*, then "the rights of the vast majority will be guaranteed." But "if rightists or right opportunists are in control, these organs and enterprises [i.e., the state and production] may change qualitatively."[80] Instead of seeing political ideologies as a product of the class relations governing society, Mao now argued the reverse: the ideas of the people in charge determine the class nature of society.

Mao's first attempt to put this perspective into practice came in 1963, with the Socialist Education Movement. The mobilization not only sent students and intellectuals to the countryside to work alongside peasants—thereby easing unemployment and population pressures in the cities—but also encouraged workers and peasants to critique the party bureaucracy. Carried out through the party apparatus, however, the effort was quickly blunted. Liu Shaoqi revised Mao's initial mandate for the mobilization, narrowed its scope, and gave party "work teams" tight control over mass activity. From his position of decreased influence, Mao seemed incapable of halting a slow slide into capitalist "restoration." Thus he planned a mass campaign in the late 1960s that would shake Chinese society to its foundations: the Cultural Revolution.

IV.

■ THE CULTURAL REVOLUTION

Mao and his allies initiated the Cultural Revolution (CR) partly to oust bureaucratic opponents but also in an earnest attempt to prevent what they saw as creeping capitalist restoration. They understood this threat in the manner formulated by Mao in the late 1950s and early 1960s: part of the continuing class struggle under socialism, fueled by reactionary ideas in the superstructure of society and vaguely defined "imperfections" in the socialist economic base. To wage this class struggle, Mao aimed to circumvent the established CCP hierarchy. But while Mao's wing of the party only intended a *cultural* revolution, they unwittingly stumbled upon a deeper reality: the explosive class contradictions generated by state capitalist exploitation.

One source of class tension stemmed from the rise of a new generation of potential bureaucrats. By the mid-1960s, the Chinese educational system was finally producing large numbers of educated youth each year, with the number of annual college graduates nearly quadrupling between 1957 and 1963, to two hundred thousand.[1] This stream of trained administrators, engineers, and technocrats differed markedly from the generation that had seized power in 1949. By comparison, less than a third of the party's district-level administrators in 1955 had reached junior middle school, and many were illiterate; among top-level administrators, only 5.7 percent had graduated college.[2] Yet the new educated youth found it nearly impossible to gain entry into the party elite: CCP membership had leveled off since the 1950s, adding fewer than a million cadres between 1959 and 1964, and older cadres continued to dominate senior positions.[3] From 1961 to 1964, the party even laid off 20 million state workers, relocating them to the countryside.[4] The doors to the party were closing.

A second source of class tension stemmed from the oppressive conditions imposed on the proletariat and peasantry. Resentment over the great famine and anti-rightist persecutions had simmered for years. Workers' real wages had remained stagnant since 1956, and peasants remained relegated by their *hukou* assignments to toil at near subsistence levels. And despite the rise of an educated stratum, the overall educational pyramid remained perilously steep, with only 3.6 percent of students making it beyond junior middle school in 1957, and all of those in urban areas.[5] Class mobility had come to a virtual standstill by the mid-1960s, just as thousands of young workers, peasants, and students were straining for leadership and recognition.[6]

These contradictions would explode in the CR, as mass movements erupted, developed their own perspectives on the situation in China, and escaped Mao's control. They would challenge the political and economic order and in some cases advocate for a new revolution, bringing the country to the brink of civil war. At the height of the unrest, Mao would be forced to crush the very movement he brought into being, just as he had a decade prior. With Mao's death in 1976, the "pragmatic" wing of the CCP could then take control of the state and lead China toward the authoritarian capitalist system we see today. In its spectacular demise, the CR represented a culmination of the dynamic that had first appeared in the Hundred Flowers period, the fruit of Mao's contradictory Stalinist critique of Stalinism.

19. Revolution Inaugurated: 1965–1966

The Cultural Revolution began in late 1965, in response to the publication of *Ra Hui Dismissed from Office*, a play that many believed was a veiled critique of Mao's dismissal of P'eng Te-Huai during the GLF.[7] A party committee was commissioned critique the play in early 1966, but when its efforts proved unsatisfactory to Mao, the group was replaced with a

"Cultural Revolution group" (CRG) positioned under the party Politburo. The CRG included top leaders from Mao's wing of the party, such as Zhang Chunqiao, Chen Boda, Mao's wife Jiang Qing, and others. In May 1966, the group's mission was broadened beyond literary critique: the CRG was to lead a "cultural revolution" to "criticize and repudiate those representatives of the bourgeoisie who have sneaked into the party, the government, the army, and all spheres of culture." This new movement aimed to defeat capitalist restoration:

> Those representatives of the bourgeoisie . . . are a bunch of counter-revolutionary revisionists. Once conditions are ripe, they will seize political power and turn the dictatorship of the proletariat into a dictatorship of the bourgeoisie. Some of them we have already seen through, others we have not. Some are still trusted by us and are being trained as our successors, persons like Khrushchev, for example, who are still nestling beside us.[8]

Students in Beijing were the first to respond when Mao's call was circulated. "Red Guard" groups formed in June 1966 at Beijing University and Tsinghua Middle School, conducting big poster campaigns against educational policy. At first, students that understood themselves as "red" targeted other students, whom they understood as "black," with public critiques. These categories reflected the mystified character of Chinese politics, wherein "revolutionary" and "reactionary" were equated with one's relationship to the party. In this case, educational policy in the 1960s differentiated between students from "red" and "black" backgrounds: "red" students included the children of party cadres in good standing, and students entering higher education from the proletariat or peasantry; "black" students included children of the deposed ruling classes, and anyone persecuted as "rightist" in previous purges.[9] While policies favored "red" students, "black" students from educated backgrounds continued to succeed in higher education. Competition between the two groups grew fierce, as the possibilities for class mobility through education narrowed.

Mao's call for cultural revolution unleashed the conflict between these two factions. "Red" students formed Red Guard groups and demanded the exclusion of "black" students from educational institutions. They called for more favorable policies toward workers and peasants, and attacked school administrators for insufficiently favoring "red" students. The Red Guard mobilization thus called simultaneously for greater class mobility for proletarian and peasant youth, and at the same time, for a new educated elite to displace its predecessor. Classes were suspended in schools across Beijing as the movement grew, and local education officials were subjected to harsh public criticism.

The disruption was too much for CCP pragmatists. In June 1966, Liu Shaoqi sent party "work teams" onto the campuses in Beijing, to rein in public criticisms. Struggle sessions were to be limited to pre-planned gatherings, and cadres would ratify targets chosen by the students. Yet Mao sided strongly with the rebellious youth, sparking an internal conflict within the party. In August 1966, he published a call to "Bombard the Headquarters" in the *People's Daily*, officially sanctioning the Red Guard movement and castigating the "white wind" that had attempted to contain it. In a letter to Red Guards at a Beijing middle school, he affirmed that it was "right to rebel against reactionaries." Mao oversaw a mass parade of Red Guard groups in Tiananmen Square, and called on police to avoid hampering Red Guard activities.

The same month the CCP Central Committee released a set of "Sixteen Articles" on the CR. Specifying the methods the movement could adopt on a mass level, the articles effectively opened the floodgates to mobilizations across the country. Yet on paper the articles themselves were not particularly radical. As in previous mobilizations, cadres were to stimulate mass activity and manage contradictions among the people. The CR aimed to root out a "handful" of "anti-Party, anti-socialist rightists" within the bureaucracy, rather than targeting the party-state in its entirety. The articles insisted that "the great majority" of party cadres were "good" or "comparatively good," and thus the movement would ultimately unify "more than

95 per cent of the cadres" behind a revolutionary political line. Finally, the campaign was in no way to interfere with the proletariat at work: "Any idea of counterposing the Great Cultural Revolution to the development of production," the document insisted, "is incorrect."

Thus the Sixteen Articles conceived of the CR mainly as an effort to wipe ideological cobwebs from the superstructure of Chinese society, and oppose a small number of cadres who had fallen under the sway of the reactionary ideas propagated by the overthrown ruling classes. "Although the bourgeoisie has been overthrown," the articles argue, "it is still trying to use the old ideas, culture, customs and habits of the exploiting classes to corrupt the masses, capture their minds and endeavor to stage a comeback." The objective of the CR was thus

> to struggle against and overthrow those persons in authority who are taking the capitalist road, to criticize and repudiate . . . the ideology of the bourgeoisie and all other exploiting classes and to transform education, literature and art and all other parts of the superstructure not in correspondence with the socialist economic base, so as to facilitate the consolidation and development of the socialist system.[10]

Despite their limited scope, the Sixteen Articles provided sanction and guidance to the CR as a mass movement. With this intervention from above, Red Guard groups sprang up in most major Chinese cities, and surged in size and activity. At the same time, Mao's wing reasserted control within the CCP. Liu Shaoqi and Deng Xiaopeng were targeted as the main revisionists in the party: Deng was removed from office, and Liu was replaced as Party Deputy Chairman by military chief Lin Piao.[11] The party leadership was soon immobilized by criticism from below and the threat of denunciation by Mao, and the Politburo effectively ceased to function. The CRG became the de facto political authority in China, directing the CR from Beijing. The movement had become a national phenomenon.

20. Red Guards in Beijing: 1966–1967

Throughout the summer and autumn of 1966, the epicenter of the CR remained in Beijing. Mao called on Red Guards to attack the "four olds": old customs, culture, habits, and ideas. In response, Red Guards posted big character posters on public streets, distributed propaganda extolling revolutionary virtues, performed street theater castigating revisionism, and criticized educational officials. Some Red Guard groups also destroyed historical artworks and cultural or religious sites. Others carried the mobilization to an extreme, targeting members of the deposed bourgeoisie and petit-bourgeoisie and their relatives. Attacks on "black" categories soon became a salient feature of the Red Guard movement.

The targets of Red Guard groups were subjected to extended criticisms before mass audiences, forced to wear placards and dunce caps announcing their crimes, held before crowds in "jet" poses, with their arms pulled behind them and their heads held low, and were often beaten if they resisted. According to police statistics, from mid-August to the end of September, Red Guards searched 33,600 homes in Beijing, resulting in at least 1,772 beating deaths.[12] Mao eventually called on the Red Guards to show restraint in their criticisms, while also maneuvering to insulate the party and the economy from disruption: in September 1966, he forbade Red Guards from raiding party offices and reminded workers and peasants to refrain from taking action and stay on the job.[13]

Red Guards also targeted sexual expression in the campaign against bourgeois culture, criticizing women for wearing makeup and skirts or engaging in extramarital affairs. When Wang Guangmei, Liu Shaoqi's wife, was accused of sexually manipulating party leaders, she was paraded before crowds in a dress, high heels, and a fake pearl necklace, indicating that she was a prostitute.[14] By contrast, Red Guards tended to perform androgyny and asexuality, with young women dressing similarly to men, avoiding contact across genders, and publicly denying sexual activity. In this way, many women entered public politics through the CR, but at the cost of abandoning struggles over specific women's issues. The Red Guards declared that "women hold up half the sky," but virtually no independent women's movements appeared during the CR, and gender issues remained muted beneath class and worker identities. The ACWF itself would be disbanded in early 1967 in an attack on "revisionist elements."

Mao greets students in Beijing, 1967.

At first, many Red Guards defined themselves and their targets using a reified notion of class known as "bloodline" theory. Extending the "red" and "black" distinction used on campuses to a hereditary principle, this theory held that one's class position was defined by the loyalty of one's parent to the party. If your parent was a war hero or prominent cadre, you were "red" and thus eligible for membership in Red Guard groups. If your parents were members of the former ruling classes or persecuted as "rightists," you were "black" and precluded from Red Guard membership. As a popular saying put it: "The father's a hero, the son's a brave lad; the father's a reactionary, the son's a bastard."[15] At first prominent party leaders such as Guang Feng and Jiang Qing sanctioned the bloodline theory, with reservations. The CRG would eventually criticize it in October 1966.

The neat battle lines of the bloodline theory began to break down, however, as the movement expanded. Demonstrations spilled outside the universities, and Red Guards began to target members of the party bureaucracy viewed as corrupt or authoritarian, in addition to "black" categories. This shift still fell within the bounds set by the Sixteen Articles, but it divided the movement nonetheless. While some Red Guard groups welcomed critiques of party cadres, others refused to attack the party in any way, limiting their attacks solely to "black" groups. Even among Red Guards who criticized the party, participants did so for different reasons. Many groups united children of the rising party elite alongside children of the proletariat and peasantry. Some sincerely sought to attack party corruption, while others aimed to oust a specific set of local party leaders and install themselves in favorable positions.

As campaigns exploded across Beijing, some Red Guard groups targeted party officials, and others mobilized to defend the officials with whom they were allied from attack. In this way a new polarization emerged, first in Beijing and then across the country: on one side were "radical" groups that targeted elements of the party apparatus, and on the other side were "conservative" groups that defended specific officials. Physical confrontations between the two flared in the streets. Their rhetoric was often indistinguishable, with both sides labeling one another "conservative" and all groups legitimizing their actions in the phraseology of Mao and the CRG.

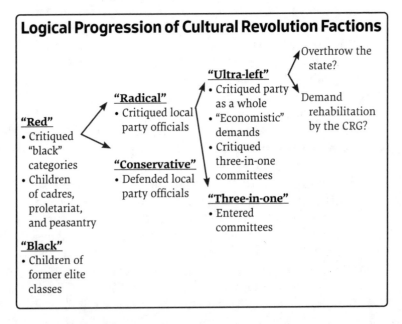

Logical Progression of Cultural Revolution Factions

"Red"
- Critiqued "black" categories
- Children of cadres, proletariat, and peasantry

"Black"
- Children of former elite classes

"Radical"
- Critiqued local party officials

"Conservative"
- Defended local party officials

"Ultra-left"
- Critiqued party as a whole
- "Economistic" demands
- Critiqued three-in-one committees

"Three-in-one"
- Entered committees

Overthrow the state?

Demand rehabilitation by the CRG?

Even among CR groups calling themselves "radical," tensions remained. Many students from worker and peasant backgrounds, and in some cases declassed intellectuals, were resentful of cadre privileges in general and thus inclined to wage broad attacks on the party bureaucracy and not merely a "handful" of officials. As the unrest grew, these young intellectuals and workers, many of whom had grown up under CCP rule, began to question the nature of Chinese society and how to revolutionize it. Gradually a revolutionary wing of the movement took shape, moving from a critique of "black" categories to a critique of a "handful" of party officials, and eventually, to a critique of the party as a whole.

Yu Luoke, a twenty-four-year-old factory apprentice, helped spark this development by publishing *On Class Origins* in January 1967. The piece offered a thoughtful critique of bloodline theory, and it circulated widely on a national level. Yu highlighted the logical fallacies of the bloodline conception: one's class position was determined by a variety of factors beyond one's family background and clearly could not be reduced to the status of one's father. He cast the bloodline system as a caste order, questioning whether there was a difference "between those with bad family backgrounds" in China, and groups such as "blacks in America, untouchables in India, and Burakumin in Japan." Crucially, Yu went on to propose that the children of cadres were becoming "a new aristocratic stratum" in Chinese society, and that bloodline theories of class legitimized their ascent.[16]

Yu's intervention marked an important shift in the movement. By raising the idea that "red" was itself a kind of caste status, Red Guards could no longer base their revolutionary credibility on their parents' party standing. At the same time, Yu's article introduced a critique, not just of a "handful" of officials but of Chinese society as a whole. Yu would later be denounced by the CRG for holding this position, arrested in January 1968, and executed in March 1970.[17] But by then the shift he inaugurated in theory would be expressed in practice. A Red Guard group named Jinggangshan at Tsinghua University, for example, studied and criticized Yu's analysis and soon broadened their critique beyond "black" students. Jinggangshan would eventually seize control of Tsinghua campus in December 1966, criticizing the "hierarchical system, cadre privileges, the slave mentality, the overlord style of work, and the bloated bureaucracy."[18]

Yet the shift to systemic critique was still not widespread. As Red Guard groups picked targets for mass criticism, they could easily be drawn into factional struggles against one party faction or in defense of another. Throughout 1966 and early 1967, most CR groups remained mired in factional battles, with the CRG backing whichever side was most strategic for Mao's wing of the party. The CR movement in Nanjing, for example, never broke out of clientelist factional disputes, or formed independent groupings opposed to the party as a whole.[19] But in the industrial stronghold of Shanghai, the story was different. There the working class emerged as a powerful independent force, with the potential to overturn the party-state itself.

21. Dual Power in Shanghai: January 1967

In late 1966, the CR leapt beyond its initial student base and found a new home in Shanghai. Already that autumn, student Red Guard groups had formed in the city, growing to nearly 150,000 members in high schools and universities. Now in November 1966, workers from seventeen Shanghai factories moved to form their own Workers General Headquarters (WGH).[20] The story of the workers' movement in Shanghai encapsulates the radical trajectory of the CR: the initial polarization between "conservative" and "radical" groups gave rise to a series of clashes and splits, out of which crystallized worker groups increasingly conscious of their own interests and goals independent of the party.

The WGH won recognition in Shanghai after a thousand workers commandeered a series of trains bound for Beijing. Zhang Chunqiao, a member of the CRG, was forced to sanction the group as an official CR organization, and provide it with material support. The WGH then established a series of divisions across the city, and worker "brigades" flocked to the umbrella organization. In factories, public utilities, and transport hubs, workers launched big poster campaigns and public criticisms of party officials under the auspices of the WGH.[21] By the following year the organization boasted over seven hundred thousand members, and their numbers continued to grow.[22] Yet as soon as workers began to criticize party officials, a rival group of conservative workers formed the "Scarlet Guards" to defend the local Shanghai party committee. Shanghai's Scarlet Guards gained four hundred thousand members shortly after their founding.[23]

A confrontation between the two worker blocs soon exploded, in the "Kangping Road" incident of December 1966. Thirty thousand Scarlet Guards surrounded the mayor's compound on Kangping Road, demanding recognition as an official CR group, only to be met by one hundred thousand workers from the WGH. Street battles ensued, spreading to other parts of the city and lasting a full day. The clashes injured hundreds, led to over ninety hospitalizations, and delivered a decisive defeat to the conservatives. The Scarlet Guards' leaders were detained and handed over to the police, and some were subjected to mass criticisms.[24] Defeated on the streets and denied "official" CR status by the CRG, the Scarlet Guards were forced to disband.

The conflict between the WGH and the Scarlet Guards, and others like it around the country, was essentially a proxy battle between the party factions with which the two groups were aligned. Both sides worked to curry favor with the CRG and sanction their faction against the other. Many CR conflicts were cast in this mold at first. However, with the conservative wing decisively defeated in Shanghai, this initial struggle quickly gave rise to new oppositions within the triumphant "radical" camp itself. The process began in the winter of 1966–67, when workers mobilized for their own interests in growing antagonism with the party as a whole, in what became known as the "wind of economism."

Used as a pejorative label by Maoist cadres, the "wind of economism" referred to the tendency for Shanghai workers to form issue-oriented CR groups. No longer targeting individual party members for ideological attacks, these groups shifted to making demands on the state for legal recognitions, wages, and benefits. Of the 354 Shanghai Red Guard groups later labeled "economistic," most consisted of workers from the highly exploited sectors of Chinese society: low-wage workers; rural workers who had been sent to the countryside after the GLF and now demanded *hukou* status in Shanghai; and many temporary and contract workers from the countryside (a cheap labor pool in China's cities then as now) who demanded urban status, protections, and wages.[25] In December 1966, Shanghai's embattled mayor granted a series of wage reforms and job reclassifications to these groups. Within a few months, workers had extorted over a million yuan from the state in the form of increased wages, insurance and welfare benefits, and subsidies for travel and food. They also seized housing: over five days from December 1966 to January 1967, "all the housing in the city that had been awaiting allocation was forcibly occupied."[26]

The movement quickly spilled beyond its initial focus, however, and led to a takeover of the city in its entirety. As in many cases throughout history, the social turmoil generated by the movement compelled workers to begin managing daily life themselves. Transport, water, and electricity had been hampered for weeks as a result of factional battles and strikes. Production had been disrupted in many factories. The city government was crippled, and disorganization began to appear in rail yards and public transportation. The WGH thus began coordinating production and transportation of goods, as well as public transit, through its own mass organizations. In many factories, worker-elected committees supplanted managers and party committees.[27] It was a brief moment of dual power: the existing state apparatus had been partially displaced by a new form of proletarian organization.

Zhang Chunqiao and the CRG at first scrambled to sanction the new forms of counter-power taking shape on the ground, hosting a mass rally in January 1967. Thousands gathered in central Shanghai to officially remove the existing Shanghai Party Committee and replace it with a "Shanghai People's Commune" made up of worker groups.[28] The power shift became known across China as the "January revolution" and set a new standard for CR activity. Now groups across the country envisioned not just removing individual officials but replacing the entire local party apparatus with new forms of organization. The January Revolution unleashed a wave of rebellions throughout 1967: major strikes erupted in the provinces of Chekiang, Sichuan, Kiangsi, Kweichow, and Heilongjiang, among others. Innumerable revolts unfolded in local districts and individual factories, leading to the establishment of worker committees. Full power seizures eventually took place in twenty-nine provinces and municipalities.[29] But in Shanghai, the commune wasn't permitted to last.

22. The First Thermidor

In urgent meetings with the CRG, Mao opposed the formation of the Shanghai People's Commune. At a meeting with Zhang Chunqiao and Yao Wenyuan in mid-February, Mao critiqued the seizure on practical grounds. "If the whole of China sets up people's communes," Mao asked, "should the People's Republic of China change its name to 'People's Commune of China'? Would others recognize us? Maybe the Soviet Union would not recognize us whereas Britain and France would. And what would we do about our ambassadors in various countries?"

At the same time, Mao asserted that communes were "weak when it comes to suppressing counter-revolution. People have come and complained to me that when the Bureau of Public Security arrest people, they go in the front door and out the back."[30] In the interest of maintaining China's stability within the inter-state system, and guaranteeing the state's effective monopoly on force internally, Mao called for the Shanghai commune to be disbanded.

Zhang Chunqiao imposed this decision in Shanghai in collaboration with the WGH leadership. In late February 1967, the WGH and Zhang held another mass rally, this time announcing the dissolution of the Shanghai People's Commune and the formation of a "Shanghai Revolutionary Committee" in its place. The new committee was built along a three-in-one model, which brought together representatives from worker organizations with representatives from the army and party cadres. This form of organization, an editorial in *Red Flag* declared, would be the "provisional organ of power" of the CR. By contrast, the editorial insisted, "the concept of excluding and overthrowing all cadres is absolutely wrong." Such a view was a "poisonous influence" that had been "advocated by those several people who put forth the bourgeois reactionary line," and which was unwittingly parroted by well-intentioned sectors of the movement.[31]

The three-in-one model became the primary form through which Mao co-opted the radical upsurge of the CR. The committees allowed the party to admit insurgent forces into the governing apparatus, while outweighing them numerically with cadres and military officials loyal to the party center. In many cases, officials who had been criticized and ousted months before were rehabilitated to serve on them. Throughout 1967 three-in-one committees were established in provinces, cities, factories, and schools. In some cases they even served as a preemptive move to blunt mobilization from below: in Nanjing, local rebel groups declined to seize power at an official's request, insisting that they weren't prepared to run the province. Assured that "power seizure" would only involve them supervising incumbent officials, the rebels replied, "if that's what power seizure means, we can do it."[32]

In Shanghai, the various three-in-one committees now running the city contained large numbers of workers. But as one committee member complained, workers were usually "put in charge of secondary matters and administrative details . . . few handled political work." The majority of leadership posts were reserved for party cadres or, at best, workers who were party members. At the Shanghai Bureau of Light Industry, worker representation was far less than a third: only 9.6 percent of leadership posts were filled by rebel workers, and in some committees the figure was as low as 4.1 percent.[33] In some cases, emerging worker leaders were quickly recruited into the party apparatus.

With this structure in place, Mao's wing of the party moved against the "wind of economism." Mao believed "economistic" groups were a creation of capitalist roaders in the party, who hoped to "buy off" the movement with material gains. In casting their demands as "economistic," he ignored the views of rebel workers and the causes of their grievances and labeled them reactionaries based on his assumption that the party's political leadership was sacrosanct. The CRG thus initiated a crackdown, forcing many single-issue rebel groups in Shanghai to disband and avoid imprisonment. The WGH leadership supported the crackdown, releasing a flyer that stated "we are rebelling against a small handful of authorities taking the capitalist road, rebelling against the reactionary bourgeois line, and not primarily over 'money.'"[34] City agencies were concerned with money, however: they demanded workers return the funds disbursed to them, and eventually recouped 488,000 yuan back into the hands of the state.[35] The message was clear: it was acceptable to choose sides behind party factions, but it was not acceptable to level independent demands on the party as a whole.

The February repression finalized a split within "radical" ranks, between groups content to critique a "handful" of party leaders and gain acceptance under three-in-one committees, and others who pursued an independent critique of the CCP and Chinese society. In Tsinghua University in Beijing, for example, the Jinggangshan group split over whether to accept rehabilitated cadres in the new three-in-one structures. The radical faction, most of whose members hailed from peasant and worker backgrounds, opposed the rehabilitated cadres and called for "mass supervision" of all three-in-one committees instead.[36] In many cases, splits first emerged between groups accepted into three-in-one committees and those excluded from them. In Shanghai this tendency cohered around a group known as Lian Si.

Lian Si was a group of three thousand young factory workers, who had been persecuted in the mid-1960s as a "counterrevolutionary clique" for writing slogans such as "Let's hold dance parties at once!" and "Long live women!" on factory walls. With blighted records, the Lian Si workers found themselves excluded from the three-in-one system. The group responded by arguing that "Shanghai's leadership authority is not in the hands of the proletariat," and calling for "an alliance of all revolutionary rebels in the city who were suppressed after February 5, 1967." The group established liaison posts across the city, and soon attracted all the forces left out of the new political order, or whose "economistic" demands had been sidelined by it.[37] The group called for the overthrow of the Shanghai Revolutionary Committee.

WGH-affiliated groups soon challenged Lian Si–affiliated groups in the streets. April 1967 saw 156 armed battles in Shanghai, and 140 clashes in the first week of May alone, in tandem with an uptick of violent clashes across the country.[38] In August 1967, the WGH sent thousands of combatants to attack the Lian Si headquarters at the Shanghai Diesel Engine Factory, sparking a major confrontation in which workers battled with iron bars, bricks and Molotov cocktails. By the end of the conflict, 983 were injured and 1,000 Lian Si members were taken prisoner.[39] A year earlier the conservative Scarlet Guards had been beaten on the streets; now the movement's radical wing was on the losing end. Lian Si effectively ceased to exist, and there were no further challenges to the three-in-one power structure in Shanghai.

Though defeated in Shanghai, a potentially revolutionary tendency continued to emerge across China. With each successive phase of conflict and cooptation, the most radical CR groups grew more antagonistic with the party-state, eventually crystallizing in a distinct "ultra left" wing of the movement. The "ultra left" comprised a diverse milieu of rebel groups and publications, which called variously for new organizations outside the CCP, a revolutionary split in the army, and a new revolution in China. Yet at the same time they hesitated to break with the CRG and Mao, believing the latter were on their side. In 1967–68, these developments came to a head in Hunan Province.

23. The "Wuhan Incident" and Armed Struggle: 1967

The seeds of the Hunan ultra-left were planted in Xiang River Storm and the Red Flag Army, two large coalitions coordinating across the province in a practice known as the "revolutionary link-up." Xiang River Storm was a coalition of some one million members, including students, workers from cooperative enterprises, temporary urban workers, youth returning from the countryside to demand *hukou* status, and the urban unemployed.[40] The Red Flag Army was a 470,000-strong group of disgruntled PLA veterans demanding state benefits. Both groups had been driven underground in January–February 1967, with over 100,000 of their members arrested.[41]

The CRG's crackdown and cooptation was briefly halted, however, in response to the "Wuhan incident."[42] In July 1967, conservative rebel groups backed by local military officials laid siege to rebel groups that had tried to seize power in Wuhan. Xie Fuzhi and Wang Li from the CRG traveled to the city, intending to mediate the dispute in favor of rebel forces. But when they arrived, they were promptly arrested by local military officers. The allegiances of military commanders in Wuhan now appeared unclear. Mao himself was in Wuhan at the time for an inspection tour and had to be hastily flown to Shanghai with an escort of fighter jets. Zhou Enlai then flew to Wuhan to address the situation, but local military forces surrounded the airstrip and prevented his plane from landing. For a moment, it looked as if conservative elements in the army had lost their patience with the CR and were moving toward an outright coup.

The Wuhan mutiny was quickly put down by Lin Piao, head of the military and Mao's close ally. Infantry divisions, navy gunboats, and air force units descended on the city and forced a speedy surrender. But after the incident was resolved, Mao had to address the danger of conservative forces in the army. He thus appealed to the very left-wing base he had just repressed and advocated publicly for "arming the left" and expanding the CR to target "capitalist roaders in the army" as well as the party. Mao's wife Jiang Qing openly called for the movement to begin seizing arms. Rebel groups took Mao at his word. To many across the country, it seemed Mao's call marked an official reversal of the February counterrevolution. Over the following weeks, both left- and right-wing CR groups expropriated guns from armories. In some provinces revolutionaries seized trainloads of armaments bound for Vietnam. "The lesson of the Wuhan Incident," wrote one young rebel, "is that a prerequisite for seizing power . . . is to take over the military power usurped by the handful of bourgeois representatives in the army. Otherwise, the power seizure is nothing but empty talk."[43]

Shanghai factory, 1969. The poster reads: "The working class is the main force in the Cultural Revolution. The valiant Shanghai workers rose to rebuff Liu Shaoqi's bourgeois headquarters for whipping up the evil counterrevolutionary wind of economism in an attempt to suppress the Cultural Revolution."

Shooting wars soon broke out on the streets of Chinese cities, as rebel groups engaged in armed clashes with the military and conservative factions. In Changsha, rebel groups retained control of the city's major factories after defeating conservative forces that had seized control of a gun manufacturing plant in neighboring Xiangtan.[44] In Beijing, rebels went so far as to seize the Foreign Ministry, and call on Chinese diplomatic posts across the globe to spread the revolution (thus answering in practice Mao's earlier concern about a commune's place in the international state system).[45] In August 1967 there were between twenty and thirty armed clashes every day across China. Three years later, Mao would recall: "Everywhere people were fighting, dividing into two factions. There were two factions in every factory, in every school, in every province, and in every county . . . There was massive upheaval throughout the country."[46]

The unrest reached its limit in September 1967, when Mao's wing of the party again stifled the revolutionary wave it had called into being. That month, Mao authorized the army to use armed force to defend itself while restoring order. Mao's wife Jiang Qing reversed her call for the left to seize arms, and denounced a group that had done so in Beijing—the small May 16 Group—as an "ultra-left" conspiracy bent on conducting a coup. In Hunan the military confiscated rebel arms, collecting "5,510 guns (including 280 machine guns), 28 artillery pieces, 621 rounds of artillery shell, 11,853 hand grenades, 1,077,026 rounds of bullets, and 5,573 kilograms of explosives" in one week.[47] Party directives instructed Red Guard students across the country to cease the "revolutionary link-up" and return to classes, and for rural youths to return to the countryside. Others demanded the dissolution of "mountain strongholds": class-wide organizations that spanned large geographical territories beyond party oversight.

As in Shanghai, not all rebel groups accepted the crackdown. By late 1967, the young militants in Hunan had experienced a year of power seizures, armed conflicts, and betrayals from party leaders. They began to develop their own definition of their friends and enemies.

24. *Whither China?* and the Ultra-Left

In October 1967, the groups that composed Xiang River Storm and the Red Flag Army held a conference in Changsha to establish a new, province-wide revolutionary coalition and push beyond the existing three-in-one system. The conference included over twenty groups across the province, made up of students, youth returning from the countryside, army veterans, and temporary workers. The new coalition chose the name Shengwulian (an acronym for Hunan Provisional Proletarian Revolutionary Great Alliance Committee). It numbered around three hundred thousand members—roughly the size of the entire CCP in 1940.[48] Yet many of Shengwulian's constituent groups did not seek to overthrow the state, aiming instead at specific reforms or rehabilitation by the CRG. So dependent was Shengwulian on sanction from above that the coalition cancelled its founding celebration after Zhou Enlai denounced the new group as "ultra left." Many groups abandoned Shengwulian at this point, before the alliance even got off the ground.

Other sections of the coalition began to reflect on their situation, however, and reached reach profoundly new conclusions. "Our Program," written by Zhang Yugang, a student at the South-Central College of Mining, in December 1967, argued that the CR should not limit itself to removing a "handful" of revisionist cadres inside the CCP. Instead it should target the "newly born corrupted bourgeois privileged stratum" and "smash the old state apparatus that is in the service of bourgeois privilege."[49] Similar ideas were crystallizing across the country, as newborn "ultra-left" groups circulated their perspectives in local newspapers, posters, and leaflets. The "ultra-left" current included the "Communist Group" in Beijing, the "October Revolution Group" in Shandong, the "Oriental Society" in Shanghai, the "August 5 Commune" in Guangzhou, and the "Plough Society" in Wuhan.[50]

The most prominent "ultra left" position was synthesized in the Shengwulian statement *Whither China?*, released in December 1967.[51] *Whither China?* was written by Yang Xiguang, an eighteen-year-old Hunanese student imprisoned for forty days for supporting Xiang River Storm. Yang wrote the document as a discussion piece, offering an appraisal of events since January 1967. In it, he argues the movement should establish a "People's Commune of China" modeled roughly on the Paris Commune of 1871—a course of action proven possible by the January Revolution, and the arms seizures of August 1967.

In January 1967, government and the means of production had briefly passed "from the hands of the bureaucrats into the hands of the enthusiastic working class," Yang argues, and "for the first time, the workers had the feeling that 'it is not the state which manages us; but we who manage the state.'" Later, "in the gun-seizing movement, the masses, instead of receiving arms like favors from above, for the first time seized arms from the hands of the bureaucrats by relying on the violent force of the revolutionary people themselves." This move allowed "the emergence of an armed force" organized by the people, which became "the actual force of the proletarian dictatorship . . . They and the people are in accord, and fight together to over- throw the 'Red' capitalist class."

For Yang, the events of 1967 had proven the Chinese pro- letariat had the ability to depose the existing rulers, and run society on an egalitarian basis. In contrast with Mao's claim in 1966 that only a "handful" of party cadres were reaction- ary while "the great majority" were good, Yang insists that "90 percent of the senior cadres . . . already formed a privi- leged class." Yang uses the term "'Red' capitalist" to describe the enemies of the revolution, and argues that since 1949, the relation between the party and the masses has "changed from relations between leaders and the led, to those between rulers and the ruled and between exploiters and the exploited." Now a "Red capitalist class" rules a social order "built upon the foundation of oppression and exploitation of the broad masses of people." "In order to realize the 'People's Commune of China,'" Yang argues, it is now "necessary to overthrow this class."

Yang refuses using three-in-one committees as a path to proletarian power, because they "will inevitably be a type of regime for the bourgeoisie to usurp power, in which the army and local bureaucrats will play a leading role." Furthermore, Yang notes that "some of the armed forces . . . have even become tools for suppressing the revolution," and thus the only option for the movement is to foment a split in the army, and launch a new armed struggle. "A revolutionary war in the country is necessary," he argues, "before the revolutionary people can overcome the armed Red capitalist class." Revolutionaries must build on the "ultra left" groupings scattered across the country, and form a new "Mao Tse-tung-ism party" separate from the existing CCP.

Whither China? displays confusions about Mao's role in the CR. Yang repeatedly characterizes Mao's efforts to contain proletarian movement as temporary tactical retreats, and selects the most revolutionary of his vacillating positions to justify an "ultra-left" stance. Nevertheless, Yang's document represents the intellectual fruit of two years of massive class struggle on the part of the Chinese proletariat, and the clearest expression of the liberatory possibilities of the Chinese Revolution. From targeting a "handful" of party officials, to Yu Luoke's critique of the party as a privileged "caste," the "ultra-left" now viewed the party-state as a ruling class exploiting the proletariat. Through mass protests, armed clashes and power seizures, the mass movement had achieved a new level of clarity regarding the class relations in Chinese society, and produced a new generation of revolutionaries striving for independence from the CCP. Reflecting on this arduous process, Yang writes:

> This is the first time the revolutionary people have tried to overthrow their powerful enemies. How shallow their knowledge of this revolution was! Not only did they fail consciously to understand the necessity to completely smash the old state machinery and to overhaul some of the social systems, they also did not even recognize the fact that their enemy formed a class.

After the publication of *Whither China?*, Yang and his milieu produced further documents on revolutionary organization, and investigated the situation of workers and peasants across Hunan Province.[52] The Wuhan-based "Plow Society" reaffirmed the class analysis put forth by Yang, calling for the formation of a new revolutionary party, and analyzing the different factions in the CR movement. The group's "inaugural declaration" stated:

> Political climbers are fighting each other to secure their seats. . . . But there are also a large number of revolutionary whippersnappers who have been making unremitting efforts to prepare "weapons" and "ammunition" for battles in the future. Those who desire nothing but being part of the officialdom . . . will eventually be abandoned by the people. The hope of our country is placed in those who

are willing to seek truth and study hard to understand the current moment.[53]

The young leaders of the ultra-left had little time to "seek truth and study hard," however, as they soon came under attack from above.

In January 1968, CRG leaders Jiang Qing, Kang Sheng, Yao Wenyuan, Chen Boda and Zhou Enlai unanimously condemned Shengwulian as "counterrevolutionary," and called for mass criticism of *Whither China?* (ironically allowing the document to circulate widely across the country). Li Yuan, a general in Changsha, denounced Shengwulian as a "big hodge-podge of social dregs" composed of "landlords, rich peasants, counter-revolutionaries, rightists, unrepentant capitalist roaders, KMT leftovers, and Trotskyist bandits." Mao himself began using the term "Shengwulian-style hodgepodge" as an epithet for the groups who had emerged from the factional battles of 1967 seeking autonomy from the state.[54]

"Stop the armed struggle at once!" 1967 poster from Qingdao Municipal General Command of the Revolutionary Trade Unions.

Shengwulian's intellectual leaders fled into hiding: Yang went underground but was soon captured in Wuhan and arrested, while his mother was captured and driven to suicide by repeated mass criticisms.[55] Zhou Guohi, a contemporary of

Yang's, was captured, beaten, and subjected to dozens of mass denunciations.[56] By February 1968 Shengwulian was effectively destroyed, and its constituent groups disbanded. A Hunan provincial revolutionary committee, built on the three-in-one model, was put in place in April without significant resistance. By August, Wuhan's "Plow Society" was also disbanded, and its leaders imprisoned.[57]

Similar events unfolded across the country. In July 1968, Mao dispatched "Mao Zedong Thought Propaganda Teams" to take control of Tsinghua University in Beijing, where the Jinggangshan group opposed the university three-in-one committee. The teams, supervised by military officers and composed of workers who were largely party members, disbanded student groups and established a three-in-one committee to run the campus under their supervision.[58] Now Mao played the role of Liu Shaoqi, suppressing the student movement from the party center. Cities, universities, and factories across the country were similarly stabilized through crackdowns and three-in-one committees, even though wildcat strikes would continue to disrupt production into 1970. These developments marked the end of mass proletarian initiative under Mao's rule.

25. The *Shanghai Textbook* and Capitalist Ideology

After the movements of 1967–68 were repressed, Mao and the CRG worked to consolidate what they saw as the gains of the period. One part of this effort was the publication of materials that popularized Mao's ideas within the party. In 1974, the CCP published a textbook entitled *Fundamentals of Political Economy* as part of a Youth Self-Education series, which summarized Mao's understanding of socialist transition and economics. The manual has been republished in the United States under the title *Maoist Economics and the Revolutionary Road to Socialism: The Shanghai Textbook*, and today serves as a reference point for many Maoists. While a close reading of the entire *Shanghai Textbook* is not possible here, we can briefly examine it as a synthesis of Mao's understanding of the proper management of state capitalism.

The *Textbook* opens with a schematic model of how revolutions unfold. First, a revolutionary upsurge demolishes the

bourgeois superstructure of a given society, establishes a socialist economic base, and inaugurates the period of socialism or
"lower" communism, as delineated in Marx's 1875 *Critique of the
Gotha Program*.[59] Once industries are nationalized, the "establishment of the system of socialist public ownership" constitutes a
"fundamental negation of the system of private ownership,"[60] at
which point "all laborers become masters of enterprises."[61] The
textbook doesn't describe this mastery in qualitative terms but
rather asserts and assumes it, premised on the idea that public
property predominates in society.

The process of socialist transition doesn't stop at nationalization, however. Following nationalization, the new "socialist relations of production" must also "undergo a process of
development" and improvement.[62] Along the way, society
encounters contradictions "between the superstructure and
the economic base under socialism": bad habits and ideas
from the old society linger in mass consciousness; members
of the overthrown classes maneuver to reenter positions of
power; and bureaucratic work methods and other "imperfections" hinder state production. All these factors hold back "the
consolidation, improvement, and further development of the
socialist economic base." Thus the party must develop ways
to address these contradictions, and "make the socialist superstructure better serve the socialist economic base" in turn.[63]
Thankfully, the *Textbook* argues, contradictions under socialism
are "not antagonistic and can be resolved one after another by
the socialist system itself."[64]

According to the *Textbook*, contradictions remain non-
antagonistic under socialism because the party in state power
is synonymous with the proletariat's mastery over society.
"Ultimately it should be the laborers themselves" who organize the production process, the *Textbook* admits, but "naturally,
this does not mean that all the laborers directly organize and
manage production." Instead "the broad masses of laborers
appoint representatives through the state and the collective,
or they elect representatives to organize production,"[65] and
these appointed and elected managers then "rely on the masses"
while carrying out their duties.[66] The "reliance" of leaders upon

led depends not on specific mechanisms of authority and power, the *Textbook* argues, but rather upon the political line of the cadres in command: "when the leadership of the socialist economy is in the hands of genuine Marxists, they can represent the interests of the workers . . . in owning and dominating the means of production."[67] "The crux of judging who controls the leadership of the socialist economy" thus "lies in what line is being implemented by the departments of the enterprise in charge of production."[68]

With this formulation, Maoist theory comes full-circle, from a Marxist conception in which the social relations of production and reproduction determine the character of a society, to a bourgeois conception in which the ideas, intentions, and subjective aspirations of those in power do so. The *Textbook*'s embrace of philosophical idealism is, in turn, an extension of the substitutionist assumptions of its authors: the class nature of society is determined by the political line the party imposes, and not by the practical mastery of masses of workers over society, precisely because the party is presumed to represent the interests of the proletariat by default. Unfortunately, the claim that party cadres were "appointed" or meaningfully influenced by workers, or that managers "relied on the masses" while administering state capitalism, is mere rhetoric. As we have seen, the CCP did not rely on the masses in order to govern China but rather on their power over the reproduction of society, guaranteed through their control of production and their use of specialized armed groups to maintain this arrangement.

With substitutionist and idealist assumptions firmly in place, the *Textbook* can confidently instruct cadres in the proper administration capitalist accumulation. Nowhere is this clearer than in Chapter 5, entitled "Develop Socialist Production with Greater, Faster, Better, and More Economical Results." Here the authors admit that "the commodity still has use value and value, that is, a dual nature" under socialism, and that "the economic law of commodity production is still the law of value."[69] Just as in capitalist society, socialist production "is a unity of this direct social labor process and the value-creation process."[70] How, then, does socialist production differ from capitalist production? The distinction, the *Textbook* argues, is that under state socialist regimes the law of value can be carefully applied and controlled:

> Under conditions of socialist public ownership, the law of value has a two-fold effect on socialist production: on the one hand, if utilized correctly, it can have the effect of actively promoting the development of production; on the other hand, as the law of commodity production, it is, in the final analysis, a remnant of private economy.[71]

Interestingly, the *Textbook* offers vague instructions to "restrict its negative, destructive effects," but never specifies what these negative effects consist of.[72] Thus the authors are silent on whether the existence of capitalist value reflects the presence of capitalist social relations with their own dynamics, and they provide no way to distinguish when value production under "socialism" succumbs to the capitalist drive to accumulate.

At one point, the *Textbook* insists that commodity production under socialism "is fundamentally different from capitalist private production"[73] because it is "conducted to directly meet social needs," carried out "in a planned manner," and is greatly reduced in scope.[74] Under this system

> the labor of the laborer, as concrete labor, transfers and preserves the value of the means of production used up in the production process. As abstract labor, it creates new value. Should this new value created by the producer belong entirely to the producer himself? No. To realize socialist expanded reproduction and to satisfy the diverse common needs of the laborers, society must control various social funds. . . . Therefore, in socialist society, the new value created by the producer must be divided into two parts. One part is at the disposal of the producer himself. It constitutes the personal consumption fund of the producer and is used to satisfy the personal living requirements of the producer. Another party constitutes various social funds: this social net income is at the disposal of society and is used

to further develop socialist production and to satisfy the various common needs of the masses of laboring people.[75]

Here the *Textbook*'s authors describe a fundamentally capitalist economy. Proletarians alienate their labor, and in doing so, produce use-values in the form of commodities bearing capitalist "value." This "value" is then allocated by the state, in money form, according to various considerations—but all while expanding the system of alienated labor and commodity production. The authors insist that this state of affairs differs qualitatively from capitalism. But the logic they describe is identical to the capitalist system that exists across the world, in more or less social democratic, and more or less statist, forms.

The *Textbook* insists socialist production operates with some other purpose than the self-expansion of value. "Under capitalism," its authors argue, "capital is value that generates surplus value, and the value category reflects the exploitative relations of capital over hired labor." But under socialism

> Capital funds . . . are that part of the accumulated state wealth used for production and operation. The use of these funds by the enterprise in production and operational activities follows the requirements of the fundamental socialist economic law of the satisfaction of the ever-increasing needs of the state and the people and serves expanded reproduction.[76]

Contrary to the unsupported assertions of the *Textbook*'s authors, the use of capital funds to continually expand production, thereby satisfying public and state needs while also accumulating value, is exactly what capitalism does. This "dual nature" of the production process is not a characteristic of socialism but instead reflects the exploitative relations of production predominating in society. Like a social democratic prime minister who aims to balance "productivity" with social spending, or a "progressive" CEO balancing ethics with profits, the state capitalist managers addressed by the *Textbook*'s authors must also grapple with this duality. This tension hardly makes them socialist. Rather, it makes them quintessentially capitalist.

Simply factoring human needs into the drive to accumulate does not abolish capitalism. Nor does the practice of central planning transform the relations of production in society. The *Shanghai Textbook* overlooks these contradictions, and so simply instructs cadres in managing state capitalist exploitation. This economic system was the altar on which a generation of militants, steeled in the CR and sincere in their aspiration for a free society, was sacrificed.

26. Twilight of Possibility: 1976

A range of bureaucratic intrigues and small-scale conflicts took place in China after 1968, which cannot be explored here in depth. In April 1969, the CCP was reconstituted at its Ninth Congress and moved to establish order in China. Military chief Lin Piao gradually gained a greater role in national affairs, partly under the pressure of border skirmishes with the USSR in 1969–70 that threatened to plunge the region into war. Yet while Mao pursued diplomatic relations with the United States to strengthen the economy and check Soviet aggression, others in his party preferred a military orientation toward the USSR and a greater role for the army in maintaining domestic order. Tensions between Mao and Lin grew, until the latter's followers attempted an abortive coup in 1971, and Lin died in a plane crash fleeing the country.[77] Mao was left with no clear successor, and his health began to deteriorate: already weakened by ALS (also known as Lou Gehrig's disease), he suffered a stroke in 1972 and was removed from the public eye.

Party-led campaigns continued in the 1970s, but none were allowed to threaten the state on the level of 1967. At the same time, the gains won by the proletariat during the CR were gradually institutionalized and defanged. In 1973, the WGH in Shanghai was incorporated into the preexisting ACFTU.[78] Party membership surged as the CCP absorbed a generation of leaders into its ranks, adding 7.8 million new cadres between 1969 and 1973.[79] Production too was reorganized. In 1971, French academic Charles Bettelheim toured several Chinese factories, observing how production was carried out. At the time of his visit, the General Knitwear Factory in Beijing was run by a committee of party members subject to election. The earlier party committee had been abolished in 1966, but this new body was established 1969 after the ultra-left was repressed. Below it stood a revolutionary committee built along the three-in-one model, which implemented the revolutionary line as defined by the party committee. The two leadership groups were closely entwined, with "the leading members of the party committee" also serving as "the leading members of the revolutionary committee."[80]

Apart from these bodies stood an assortment of "worker management teams," the only groups in the factory composed entirely of workers and elected by them. The teams had been formed in February 1969 as a way for workers to critique "unreasonable rules,"[81] and were intended to "act as a control" on the other bodies. However, Bettelheim was informed, "the viability of the workers' management teams" was "still under discussion."[82] Ultimately, the teams were phased out entirely. In 1971, factories across China were placed under the control of party committees, superseding the three-in-one committees that had themselves co-opted worker insurgency just a few years before.[83] In 1973, all worker management teams were placed under the control of the ACFTU.[84]

In the international arena, the CCP began to act more like a self-interested capitalist state. After breaking ties with the USSR, China had increased trade with Japan and Hong Kong-Macau, and selectively traded with Western countries such as West Germany for industrial goods. Until 1959, 65.3 percent of Chinese foreign trade had been conducted with the USSR; between 1960 and 1971, 56.1 percent went to Asian countries alone. After Mao welcomed Nixon to China in 1971, trade with Western countries tripled, making up 24.1 percent of foreign trade by 1972.[85] In tandem with these economic shifts, Mao began naming Soviet "social imperialism" as the main threat to world socialism and advocated a "Three Worlds" theory that considered the unaligned Third World the main revolutionary force on the planet.

With this orientation the CCP pursued a disastrous foreign policy. In 1971, the Chinese government lent military support to the Sri Lankan state against a Trotskyist uprising, killing thousands. The same year, it opposed the independence of Bangladesh from Pakistan, in order to prevent the formation of a Soviet-aligned state in its sphere of influence. In 1973, the Chinese government rushed to recognize the new Pinochet regime, after the Soviet- and Cuban-oriented Allende government was overthrown in a coup. In 1975 it supported UNITA, an Angolan political party also backed by the United States and the apartheid regime in South Africa, in order to prevent Soviet- and Cuban-backed MPLA guerillas from gaining power in the Angolan civil war. There is no evidence that Mao opposed any of these interventions.

Domestically, a large underground reading movement continued after the crackdowns of 1967–68, leading to a wave of mass activity in the mid-1970s. In 1974, a party-sponsored campaign against cadre privileges led to strikes and worker actions, which the party was forced to quell in April.[86] That autumn, the Li Yizhe group released a big poster entitled "On Socialist Democracy and the Legal System," critiquing the bureaucratic ruling class and calling for political freedoms.[87] Mass unrest then broke out in March and April of 1976, when crowds used memorial ceremonies for the late Zhou Enlai to wage protests against the CRG in cities across the country. Up to two million people gathered to lay wreaths and big posters in Tiananmen Square criticizing party leaders. Some posters even criticized Mao himself in veiled forms, declaring "we want premier Zhou, we don't want Franco [i.e., Mao], and even less the Empress Dowager [Jiang Qing]."[88] When officials ordered the wreaths and posters removed, crowds overturned vehicles and set a police station on fire before being dispersed with clubs.[89]

None of the 1970s mobilizations matched the mass power of 1967, however, or aimed at the revolutionary overthrow of the state. Instead protests and publications increasingly focused on the CRG and cast their concerns in terms of political rights. Thus when Mao died in September 1976, his successor Hua Guofeng easily arrested the CRG leadership (the so-called Gang of Four composed of Mao's wife Jiang Qing, Zhang Chunqiao, Yao Wenyuan, and Wang Hongwen) and the Chinese working class sat on the sidelines. Two years later, a newly rehabilitated

Deng Xiaopeng rose to power and began a series of sweeping capitalist reforms. The Maoist era was over.

The CR demonstrated the internal incoherence of the politics Mao developed from the Yenan period through the Sino-Soviet split. Unclear as to the source of class conflicts in state capitalist society, Mao framed the movement in terms of loyal "rebels" against a "handful" of capitalist roaders in the party. These terms ultimately proved incoherent, leading to waves of factionalization as the class content of the movement emerged. Though Mao was theoretically committed to revolutionizing Chinese society through mass mobilization, he nonetheless prevented these movements from developing their own autonomous capacities to govern society and displace the state. Mao in 1968 vacillated just as much as in 1957. Once again, his actions led to a handover of power to the right.

The "ultra-left" of the CR, on the other hand, was hampered by its close relationship to state power. Many CR groups were launched with the sanction and material support of party leaders, and they lacked the ability to maintain momentum and organization in antagonism with the state. Most drew their theoretical categories and political rhetoric from Mao and the CRG and only haltingly developed their own independent analysis of the situation. Lacking theoretical clarity as to who their friends and enemies were, most groups possessed only a vague idea of the kind of struggle that awaited them. Many groups fragmented in the face of state repression and scrambled to win rehabilitation from the CRG. Despite the visionary achievements of the young militants of the "ultra left," the movement they championed was crushed.

The end of the CR marked the breaking point of Maoist politics. Carried to their extreme, Mao's simultaneous commitments to Stalinist assumptions and mass mobilization against capitalist restoration led to a dead end. The price of this failure was thousands injured and killed, thousands more confused and demoralized, and capitalist exploitation for decades to come.

V.

■ CONCLUSIONS

Between the founding of the CCP in 1921, and the death of Mao in 1976, lay five decades of struggle and politics that shaped the twentieth century. Today's revolutionaries have much to learn—positive and negative—from the struggles of the Chinese proletariat and peasantry, party cadres and military units, and the actions of the CCP leadership. This book has merely scratched the surface of such an investigation, but it is now possible to draw a few conclusions about the conditions that generated Mao's politics and the applicability of those politics today.

27. Was China State Capitalist?

Many of Mao's ideas concern the proper management of economy, politics, and mass mobilizations by revolutionaries in state power. Any account of Maoism must therefore include an assessment of the kind of society Mao sought to direct, the contradictions this society presented, and how Mao's ideas grappled with these issues. In line with many anarchist and anti-state communist critics of Marxism-Leninism, I argue that the society Mao and the CCP put in place, and which they struggled to steer toward communism, can best be described as "state capitalist."

The term "state capitalism" has been used in many different historical contexts. In Russia in the 1920s, anarchists such as Alexander Berkman and Voline, and left communist groups such as Gavril Myasnikov's Worker's Group, used the term to describe the kind of exploitative political and economic system they saw emerging in the wake of the Russian Revolution. Lenin used the term positively in the same period, to describe the method the Bolsheviks would use to industrially develop Russia under Bolshevik control, while preventing the return of the overthrown ruling classes to power. Marxists throughout the twentieth century—such as Anton Pannekoek, Paul Mattick, C.L.R. James, Raya Dunayevskaya, Tony Cliff, Hillel Ticktin, and the Aufheben group—have since worked to develop the term theoretically, in order to grapple with the Soviet experience, and illuminate its implications for revolutionary movements yet to come.[1]

At its most basic level, state capitalism, like all forms of capitalism, entails the continual separation of human beings from our objective conditions of labor, on an ever-increasing scale. "Labor" in this sense is a broad category, entailing almost any kind of creative activity. Labor's "objective conditions" include everything we interact with in order to create new things: raw materials, tools, and machines, but also the food, drink, clothing, and so on needed to sustain our labor. In order to perpetuate itself, every human society must continually recreate the objective conditions of labor in some form. Each society does so through specific kinds of social relations, which in turn imbue the things people create with functions and meanings within that society.

In capitalist society our labor is alienated from us, and the things we create are alienated in turn. Thus Marx writes that labor under capitalism "assumes the form" of wage labor, conducted under the direction of a boss, in exchange for a money wage. The machines and raw materials we manipulate "assume the form" of capitalist private property, belonging to an owner and employed for his purposes. The material use-values we produce "assume the form" of commodities, sold by our employers for money, at a standard of value that remains roughly uniform throughout society. Under these conditions, our labor is turned against itself. We create commodities, capital, and capitalists that dominate over us in turn and ensure the reproduction of our alienated condition on an expanded scale. Chinese state capitalism displayed this fundamental dynamic, even though the role of the state in directing the economy, and the forms of state property through which accumulation operated, lent it a particular character different from other advanced capitalist countries.

Chinese workers produced capital, and were dominated by it. They did not control the means of production they operated, nor did they enjoy free access to the means of subsistence they produced: to access the former they needed to work for wages under a boss, and to access the latter they needed to purchase commodities on the market. While workers did participate in management committees alongside party cadres at some points in the Maoist era, their input remained limited. Generally they decided how to best execute economic plans formulated from above, or offered feedback on plans over whose final content they had little control. They were excluded from the central decisions shaping social reproduction: the division of use-values between consumption and further production, the distribution of the social product into different areas of production, and coordination between these areas.[2] Instead this control lay with cadres at the head of individual enterprises, provinces and the central government, who acted as managers and administrators of capital.

Proletarians and peasants received wages in exchange for their alienated labor. In the cities, workers received wages according to the pay grades set by the state. In the countryside, peasants experienced what Marx described as "formal subsumption": their labor process remained similar to what had existed before the revolution, but their inputs and outputs were now measured in money terms, and they were paid with a mix of money and in-kind payments (also tracked in money terms) in relation to productivity. In both cases, workers received back a portion of their social product not through a system of collective free distribution but in the form of money, which they then used to purchase the use-values expropriated from them. For peasants, in-kind wages could be directly consumed or sold on local markets in order to convert them into currency.

On the surface, little capitalist property existed in Mao's China, since the vast majority of industrial enterprises and farms were not owned as the private property of individuals (with exclusive control over their use, sale, and the profits) but were rather the property of the state or collective. However, the juridical form taken by social relations is a separate thing from these relations themselves.[3] As the twentieth century has demonstrated, capital need not always appear in the form of individual private property in order to function as capital, and accumulation can operate smoothly through many forms of collective and public property as well. Marx recognized this possibility in Volume III of *Capital*, when he explored the process through which capital becomes centralized and socialized, assuming new property forms in turn.

In the 1870s, Marx observed the rise of large monopoly firms, finance capital, and joint stock companies. He was struck that the functions of ownership, oversight, and management previously carried out by a single capitalist were now being broken up and distributed across multiple individuals. Now managers oversaw the production process in return for a "wage of administration," while financiers and stockholders passively owned shares of profits.[4] Marx believed joint stock companies, in which capital is no longer the private property of an individual but rather the common property of "associated capitalists," marked a profound shift: capital "directly assumes here the form of social capital in opposition to private capital. This is the abolition of capital as private property within the limits of the capitalist mode of production itself."[5] Marx even imagined the possibility that capital could be centralized under the state apparatus, with the "state itself as capitalist producer [with] its product as a commodity."[6] His conjectures were based on limited empirical data but were realized in the twentieth century in many forms: cooperatives, land trusts, monopoly corporations, joint stock companies, and the state capitalist regimes that operated in his name.

Beneath their legal status as state and collective property, enterprises in Mao's China still functioned as capitals. Enterprises served as "units of account," keeping their own books and tracking production costs and profits. The standard "unit of account" in urban areas was the industrial firm, while in rural areas it was generally the production brigade or, at the height of the GLF, the commune. Profits were divided between different agents of capital, much like in large corporations with financiers and stockholders. Firm managers were allowed to take a first cut, to cover capital expenditures and replenish welfare funds. Provincial and national bureaucrats would then appropriate the lion's share of profits for the state budget and the Central Bank. Finally, local bureaucrats could retain any remaining "surplus profits" for local spending, some of which could be reinvested in the most productive enterprises in the area.[7]

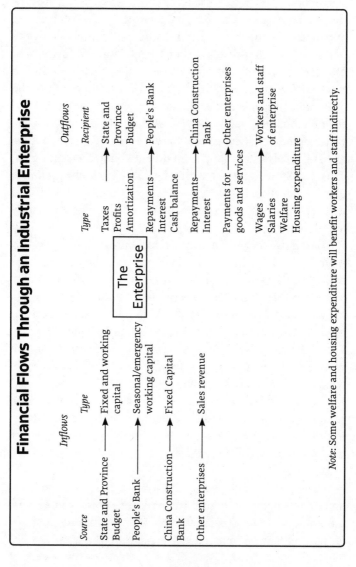

Financial Flows Through an Industrial Enterprise

Inflows

Source	Type
State and Province Budget	Fixed and working capital
People's Bank	Seasonal/emergency working capital
China Construction Bank	Fixed Capital
Other enterprises	Sales revenue

The Enterprise

Outflows

Type	Recipient
Taxes / Profits / Amortization	State and Province Budget
Repayments / Interest / Cash balance	People's Bank
Repayments / Interest	China Construction Bank
Payments for goods and services	Other enterprises
Wages / Salaries / Welfare / Housing expenditure	Workers and staff of enterprise

Note: Some welfare and housing expenditure will benefit workers and staff indirectly.

Enterprises competed to accumulate capital more efficiently than one another, though this competition was more bureaucratic and less market-mediated than in advanced capitalist societies. In the latter, firms fight to seize market share from competitors and drive each other out of business. In Mao's China, enterprises sold commodities on domestic and international markets, but they also faced controls over what and how they could produce and depended on the state for financing and material support. Enterprises would be shut down by the bureaucracy if they displayed consistently low productivity, or produced costly and defective commodities, and thus failed to meet market standards (this occurred in the aftermath of the GLF, for example). Successful enterprises would be lauded and their methods popularized. But overall, enterprises with widely varying productivity rates could survive for long periods of time, and still receive state support in order to build their industrial capacity. State capitalism thus facilitated the expansion of China's industrial base in absolute terms, even as it established weak competitive mechanisms that limited the system's ability to attain further leaps in productivity.[8]

From the perspective of individual bureaucrats, their class mobility depended partly on market performance, but more so on their standing with the higher-level officials who interpreted this performance. Thus cadres vied to exceed the goals of state production plans and contribute to the competitiveness of Chinese state capital as envisioned by party leaders. This process yielded an elaborate status system within the party, which distinguished between "state" and "local" cadres (who oversaw urban state-owned and rural collectively-owned capital accumulation, respectively) and which entailed minute seniority distinctions between different generations of cadres.[9] In this way, the party served as the venue to negotiate competition and cohesion among the emerging state capitalist ruling class.

The goods produced by Chinese workers and peasants, and appropriated by enterprise managers, were sold as commodities. A variety of relatively free markets existed in Mao's China, and many commodities were sold on the world market as well. Rural markets provided a venue for the distribution of vegetables, poultry, and other perishable commodities, many of them grown on small peasant plots. Market production in the countryside accounted for around 35 percent of China's vegetable output, and in the mid-1970s provided up to 30 percent of peasant incomes.[10] In urban areas, free markets existed for a variety of commodities beyond the three hundred or so items tightly controlled by the state. Some were consumer durables such as bicycles, radios, and watches, while others were foods such as eggs and fresh fish.[11] Staple goods such as grain, cooking oil, and cotton cloth were rationed by the state, but not according to need or labor time. Rather, workers received yearly booklets with their *hukou* status that entitled them to purchase specific amounts of staple commodities in stores, in a manner similar to federal WIC food subsidies in the United States.[12] Finally, the state sold the products of nationalized firms and agricultural communes on the world market, including grains, raw materials, and eventually textile machinery for developing countries.[13]

Yet the most important commodities, such as industrial machinery and food staples, were tightly controlled by the state. By managing the production, pricing and distribution of these products, the state could shape the overall reproduction of industry and labor-power, within limits. The main mechanism of this control was the system of production plans and price controls. State plans of varying lengths—five-year, annual, quarterly, and so on—were formulated in a complex process of negotiation between cadres at all levels. Generally, central authorities would set production goals for the key commodity chains under their control, and subsidiary plans would then be formulated on provincial and local levels to help these industries achieve their goals, incorporating feedback along the way. At the end of this process, every enterprise received a set of twelve production targets it was expected to achieve. Four target categories—"output of main commodities produced," "total profit," "average size of workforce," and "total wage bill"—were made mandatory after 1957, and the rest relegated to general guidelines.[14]

After balancing projected supply and demand within provinces, the plans allowed enterprises to negotiate contracts for sales and purchases on their own initiative. While the prices of the commodities controlled by the central government remained fixed, prices at provincial or local levels were often set through bargaining and negotiation, with official prices used as mere reference points under the sway of market forces.[15] Even goods with static prices were not simply rationed according to need. Rather, price controls allowed the state to shift the location where the surplus value extracted in their production was realized as profit. For example, the state set grain prices low when purchasing harvests from the peasantry but sold portions of the same grain on the world market at global prices, thereby realizing profits in the national budget rather than on the books of production brigades.

The movement of labor-power in Mao's China was controlled through a highly regulated labor market. The *hukou* system forced proletarians to live and work in particular areas and sectors, and workers could quit jobs only at the pain of losing their assigned status. Yet at the same time, workers were also free to vie for promotions or transfers, and the state could set wages and promotion guidelines accordingly to attract workers to important sectors of production.[16] Thus a labor market continued to exist under Chinese state capitalism, and though it resembled the "internal labor markets" of monopoly corporations more than a traditional job market, its dynamics continually strained against state control. The *hukou* system itself was originally established to stem the migration of labor-power to high-paying urban zones,[17] and when policing proved incapable of fully addressing the problem, the state was compelled to regulate migrant labor through temporary and contract work—by the early 1970s, there were over ten million such workers in China.[18] In acute periods, the state was also forced to relocate of millions of Chinese workers back to rural areas.

Finally, the Chinese economy itself remained firmly embedded in the world capitalist system. Industrializing the country required selling commodities such as grains, cotton fabrics, oilseeds, and crude oil on the world market, and purchasing chemicals, fertilizers, rolled steel, and industrial machinery in turn.[19] Throughout the 1950s, primary and processed agricultural commodities made up more than 70 percent of Chinese exports, and more than 80 percent of imports were capital goods.[20] Until the Sino-Soviet split, the majority of this trade was conducted with the USSR the socialist bloc. Afterward, it was conducted with developing economies and, increasingly after Nixon's visit to China, with the United States and the capitalist West.[21] Yet in all these exchanges, commodities were bought and sold according to prevailing global prices.[22] Despite China's marginal position in the world economy prior to the 1980s, these exchanges had significant influence on state revenues and thus on the shaping of party plans and policies. Taking 1957 and 1959 as examples, I estimate the total value of exports in these years was roughly equal in magnitude to 17 percent and 14 percent of state budgetary revenues, respectively.[23]

The above account indicates that the Chinese economy under Mao was profoundly shaped by what Marxists call the "law of value." This phrase refers to a situation in which the socially recognized "value" of commodities corresponds to the socially necessary labor-time required to produce them, providing an objective standard against which all producers are compelled to measure their efforts. Certainly, the state worked to limit labor mobility, fixed prices of key goods, and subsidized certain areas of production in order to achieve rapid industrialization. But these measures did not abolish capitalist "value." Instead, they merely directed its growing domination of Chinese society.

At times, the state's role in the economy generated what the Aufheben group calls "deformations of value."[24] With limited ability to fire insubordinate or inefficient workers, set prices, or access new technologies, enterprise managers had few ways to compete with other capitals beyond simply increasing the mass of products their enterprises produced. They thus tended to churn out defective commodities or inefficient machinery: a problem Soviet economists referred to as "fictitious products" (this dynamic was most notable during the GLF, though the quality of Chinese commodities remained a problem for decades).[25] As in the USSR, state capitalism enabled rapid industrialization but gave rise to speculative bubbles in the form of commodity capital and fixed capital.[26] To overcome this internal limit required capitalist reforms under Deng Xiaoping.

Because of its essentially capitalist dynamics, and considering its statist distortions, China under Mao can reasonably be characterized as "state capitalist." "Value" as it existed in the broader capitalist world remained the form in which use-values were equated in China, the means through which production was conceptualized and coordinated, and the objective standard with which peasants, proletarians, and party bureaucrats were forced to contend. Just as the dynamics of capital accumulation shaped Chinese society, they could not help but shape Mao's ideas about the proper management of state socialism.

28. Where Did Maoism Come From?

State capitalism provided the context in which Mao developed many of his central concepts. But the roots of his perspective lay in the relationship between the CCP and the Soviet Union in the years prior to seizing power. As we have seen, a distinctly "Maoist" politics first emerged in the 1930s, as the party gained theoretical and practical independence from the Comintern. In this period Mao and his allies developed a philosophical orthodoxy, work methods, and their own strategy for achieving socialism in China. Yet many of these formulations continued to rest on Stalinist assumptions.

"Socialism in one country," from this perspective, was not a tragic necessity imposed by the failure of the world revolution but was assumed as a goal to be prized and pursued. State capitalism and nationalization were considered unproblematic methods with which to develop semi-colonial countries, after first winning leadership in the nationalist struggle, carrying a revolution in tandem with the national bourgeoisie, and gradually replacing the latter at the head of the economy. The party's right and ability to constrain the demands of women, arbitrate between the proletariat and its class enemies, constrain

autonomous class movement, and oversee exploitative relations of production was assumed without question, thus substituting the party's leadership for proletarian self-activity.
Participatory work methods, while departing from the usual
practices of Stalinist parties, did nothing to challenge these
fundamental assumptions.

After taking power in 1949, CCP cadres displaced the existing bourgeoisie as the agents of capitalist exploitation. Despite
their claims to "socialism," the party acted as a coordinating
body for the new state capitalist ruling class, politically uniting
the managers of industrial enterprises and rural cooperatives,
state banks, and planning bodies. The development they
oversaw built the country's industrial base but also required
fixing the countryside as an internal periphery and stoking
class antagonism. Mao viewed these problems with concern
but proved unable to examine and negate his own Stalinist
framework. He still believed it was possible to attain socialism in one country, and that the continued expansion of state
capitalism, under party control, would establish the basis for
a communist society.

Mao's thought from the mid-1950s to early 1960s therefore grew increasingly contradictory, embracing state capitalist
development even as it resisted the latter's effects. As is often
the case with ideology, the influence of Mao's class position on
his ideas was apparent at the level of his assumptions, and in
the issues he chose to ignore. Mao spent large amounts of time
exploring how to ameliorate the negative symptoms of capitalist relations: "commandism" by cadres managing factories, une-
venness between city and country, conflict between enterprises,
and so on. Yet he almost never examined the basis of these
symptoms in class relations. Instead he tended to deploy stock
phrases such as "the proletariat and the communist party" or
"ownership by the whole people," glossing the socialist character
of Chinese society as an assumed fact. Behind these platitudes
lay the party's actual relationship with the proletariat, and
the actual relations of production in nationalized industries,
which Mao could not examine without questioning his own
class position.

When put into practice, these ideas could only lead to contradictory outcomes. Thus Mao supported Polish dissidence against the CPSU, but sanctioned the repression of the Hungarian Revolution; he initiated the Hundred Flowers period but quickly brought it to a close with the Anti-Rightist Campaign; he called for "non-antagonistic" relations between city and countryside but demanded leaps in steel production; and he doggedly pursued the Great Leap Forward even as the project collapsed, at great cost to human life. This damaging course of action cost Mao his position of unrivaled leadership and prestige within the CCP.

When the Sino-Soviet split forced Mao to question the nature of the Soviet state, economy, and society, he did so while maintaining his faith in the "socialist economic base." Now Mao accepted the idea that a socialist transition could lead to capitalist restoration, but he still could not connect this outcome to the exploitative dynamics of state capitalism. Instead, the source of capitalist restoration lay with members of the overthrown ruling classes and leftover ideas from the old society. This had been the fate of the USSR, Mao reasoned, and it was the ultimate destiny of his opposition within the CCP. In this way, Mao was forced to jettison Marx's materialist method of analysis and explanation, and argue that the socialist or capitalist character of a given society depended on the political line of its ruling party.

Mao launched the Cultural Revolution in the late 1960s to defend China against what he considered an impending bourgeois restoration and to return himself and his allies to control of the state. Yet the ensuing rupture unleashed class tensions he was ill-prepared to confront: factional conflicts with a rising generation of educated youth, poised to displace the generation of 1949; and masses of poor students, veterans, and industrial and temporary workers at the base of the state capitalist regime. Mao responded by crushing the autonomous proletarian movement he had unleashed, just as he had in 1957. The young militants of the Cultural Revolution, visionary though they were, lacked viable autonomous organizations or a shared, coherent understanding of their class position, goals, and strategies.

Their defeat brought the insurrectionary period of the Cultural Revolution to a close. With Mao's death in 1976, the right wing of the CCP was free to take control of the country and institute a range of openly capitalist reforms.

Mao's politics thus proved as incoherent in practice as in theory. The CCP purported to represent the proletarian leadership of the Chinese Revolution but acted as an arbiter between the proletariat and peasantry and their class enemies, joined with these enemies as co-managers of production, and finally displaced them as a new ruling class under state capitalism. The party sought to overcome the USSR's shortcomings through mass movements of criticism and self-criticism, yet methodically co-opted autonomous self-activity and repressed any challenges to the organization of Chinese society. Mao subjectively aimed to prevent capitalist restoration but objectively strengthened its hold, preventing the emergence of any force capable of challenging it.

At crucial points, Mao's politics failed to provide the proletariat with a clear assessment of its position, goals, and strategies—of its friends and enemies. Instead they led to confusion, weakness, demoralization and defeat. However sincere Mao may have been as an individual, he failed at pivotal moments to carry out the tasks of those who call themselves revolutionaries. He did not defend movements that criticized the party from a revolutionary perspective. He did not split with his party when it turned against the proletariat, whether in 1927, 1948, 1957, or 1967. He did not offer the masses in motion a clear analysis of the forces with which they were contending, the transformative tasks that lay before them, and how these tasks might be accomplished. He did not fortify and push forward class struggle from within the ranks of the exploited and oppressed.

Mao's Stalinist critique of Stalinism wallowed in incoherence and could only culminate in a handover of power to the more openly capitalist wing of his party. Just as Khrushchev represented a continuation of Stalin's policies in a more adequate form, so the capitalist reforms of Deng Xiaoping represented a continuation of Mao's.

29. What Is Useful in Mao's Politics Today?

Many different revolutionary movements have interpreted and applied Mao's ideas in the years since his death. From "Mao Zedong Thought" in the 1970s New Communist Movement[27] to the "Marxism-Leninism-Maoism" synthesis put forward by the Shining Path and the Revolutionary Internationalist Movement in the early 1990s,[28] to the people's wars currently underway in India, Nepal, and the Philippines, Mao's politics have been widely taken up. Though there are political differences between these various movements, it is possible to extract from them a constellation of philosophical, strategic, and methodological concepts that form the center of gravity for much of contemporary Maoism. We can now offer a provisional balance sheet of these core concepts.

Mass line: As a general appeal for militants to engage with the thoughts of masses of people, the mass line is laudable. The method fundamentally aims for a base of workers to develop problems, questions, and ideas in dialogue with a revolutionary organization. Yet the concept's ambiguities also allow it to be applied in a populist manner, manufacturing consent for a political line imposed from the outside. This is due to the concept's vagueness about what kinds of ideas militants should solicit, how militants should engage with them, and how they should offer ideas in return. Does mass line practice simply entail cataloguing grievances, or does it include identifying the concepts and practices proletarians are already using to address them? Do militants "concentrate" mass consciousness by subsuming local struggles under a preexisting program, or by synthesizing program and strategy itself from proletarian self-activity? Without clarity on these issues, the mass line concept admits an incredibly wide range of interpretations, many of them authoritarian in character. Revolutionaries today can deepen Mao's notion of the mass line by enriching it with a theoretical understanding of how people generate ideas in the course of daily struggles and what kinds of engagement are possible with this praxis.

Protracted people's war: Mao's military works are widely read today, by revolutionary study groups as well as the U.S. Marine

Corps, with good reason. Many of his concepts are broadly applicable to revolutionary struggles. His notion that the balance of forces in war expresses the developing internal dynamics of the contending groups; his emphasis on the mobile, opportunistic character of guerilla warfare; his confidence in the ability of guerilla warfare to shift the balance of larger conflicts; and his understanding of subjective activity realizing the potentials of objective conditions, can all be drawn upon by contemporary revolutionaries. While Mao's notion of protracted war is inapplicable in contexts lacking large territories and rural populations, his overall strategic framework may be adapted at a higher level of abstraction.

Other elements, however, must be reworked in order to inform a contemporary theory of revolutionary armed struggle. Mao conceives of the army as a tool for the implementation of a political line defined elsewhere, usually by a party that mediates between contending classes. As a result, he denies the possibility that soldiers might organize democratically or debate broader politics and strategy, and severs the army from its role in realizing the revolutionary transformation of relations of production. Today's militants can best retain Mao's useful strategic concepts by reworking his conception of military organization, in a way that more closely fuses the political and military dimensions of revolutionary struggle. In developing this line of thinking, historical examples from movements across the world will be useful, including debates over military policy in the Spanish Revolution.

Dialectics: Philosophically, the same reductive materialism, empiricism, and positivism prevalent in the Stalinist tradition are at least partly duplicated in Mao's thought. Mao's "reflection theory" of consciousness denies the critical and creative faculties of the human mind and tends to reduce consciousness to the simple corollary of objective class forces. This perspective in turn provides a philosophical justification for party substitutionism: as a group of specialists, able to grasp the objective laws of society operating independent of human will, the party can direct class struggle at will according to the objective laws it must follow. The Hundred Flowers campaign and the Cultural Revolution both exemplified this view, with the party denouncing proletarian struggles as "reactionary" or "bourgeois" without examining the consciousness and activity of the movement itself. At the same time, this perspective also lays the groundwork for an eventual lapse into idealism: if Marxism is assumed to be objective scientific truth, then the class nature of the state can be determined by whether or not its leaders hold Marxist ideas.[29]

At the same time, Mao's conflation of Knowledge and Reason obscures the role of internal contradictions in the development of conceptual categories. His philosophy thus tends toward a kind of "synthetic cognition," attentive to the empirical results of practice but disinclined to examine internal contradictions within the categories that emerge from it. This tendency is particularly clear in the way Mao critiques Stalin's writings, adding a series of addendums and caveats to his framework rather than subjecting them as a whole to an immanent critique and negation.

Given the shortcomings of Mao's philosophy, militants would benefit by transforming the accessible primers in *On Contradiction* and *On Practice* in dialogue with other philosophical works. In many cases, contemporary Maoists already do this by supplementing Mao's writings with the work of other theorists, notably Louis Althusser. But based on the above account, it would be better for militants to draw on Marxist theories of culture and praxis in order to develop an account of dialectics that emphasizes the irreducibility of social consciousness to materiality, the nature of internal contradictions within categories, and the creative character of collective thought and action.[30]

Different types of contradictions: Mao's antagonistic/non-antagonistic and primary/secondary distinctions have provided useful descriptive tools for revolutionaries in the past. For example, in a 1970 speech Huey Newton drew upon Mao's categories to define the relationship between the Black Panther Party and the women's and gay liberation movements as "non-antagonistic."[31] Today these concepts could help revolutionaries to conceptualize relationships between different sections of society, as well as the salience of specific social flashpoints, but they demand further theorization in order to rise above the level of descriptive labels.

The notion of a "non-antagonistic contradiction," for example, seems to describe simple difference or conflict, without capturing the mutually presupposing and processual character of dialectical relationships. Mao can only refer to these relations as "contradictions" because he has already excluded these qualities from his notion of contradiction in general. But rather than impoverishing the notion of contradiction itself, revolutionaries today could instead reimagine Mao's notion of "non-antagonistic" relations as an un-dialectical concept, and then proceed theorize how, why, and under what conditions such relations give rise to contradictions proper.

Similarly, Mao's primary/secondary distinction offers a useful way ground the abstract notion of contradiction in concrete social formations, with different centers of power and reciprocal influence. To identify a "primary" contradiction here is to highlight a contradiction whose continual unfolding will influence all others, by virtue of the relations of power at work within its context. Still, Mao's concept is unable to tell us how contradictions may influence one another, and under what conditions they may succeed each other in positions of importance and affectivity. To do this requires a corresponding theory of power at the specific level of abstraction in which a given dialectical relation is being described, in this case class societies. Today's revolutionary militants could seek out elements of such a theory in political philosophy, and in Marx's own political writings.

United front: Mao conceives of the united front as an alliance entered into by the communist party, on behalf of the proletariat, with other classes and class fractions—including progressive sections of the bourgeoisie and the landed elite. Central to Mao's conception is the idea that by retaining its organizational autonomy in the alliance, the party can lead nationalist struggles against imperialism toward socialism. But this conception retains the same blind spots as many of the other united front formulations in the Leninist tradition. First,

Mao fails to closely examine the implications of entering into alliances with classes whose interests are not only different from those of the proletariat but are premised on the latter's exploitation. Second, his framework does not incorporate as a key variable the relationship between a revolutionary organization and its class base.

Much of the Marxist-Leninist tradition deferred these tensions by taking the party as the organizational and theoretical embodiment of the proletariat itself. As a result, the party could enter into cross-class alliances, and constrain class struggle, while keeping the ultimate interests of the working class in mind. Executing united front tactics on this basis worked to transform the party into a force dominating over the classes it purported to represent. Today's revolutionaries must reframe this understanding of tactical and strategic alliances, starting from the self-activity of the proletariat and the autonomy of this activity from any specific form of organization. From this perspective, any strategic or tactical alliance on the part of revolutionary organizations must be evaluated on the basis of its contribution to proletarian combativeness and self-organization, and the latter must take precedence over maintaining such organizational ties.

New Democracy: Mao conceived of New Democracy as a transitional strategy, in which the party takes state power in an underdeveloped context, shares it temporarily with the national bourgeoisie and progressive landed elite, and gradually supplants the latter at the head of a state capitalist economy. Maoist movements also often implement "New Democratic" governance in base areas under their control, prior to seizing power. But whether carried out as a state or a proto-state, we have seen that New Democratic strategy positions the party as an alienated power in a given territory, standing above and mediating between different classes, while laying the foundation for the future emergence of a "red bourgeoisie." In this respect it shares many shortcomings with Mao's conception of the united front.

At the same time, changes in global capital are quickly rendering New Democracy an anachronism. The strategy itself rests on the notion that, in nations oppressed by imperialism, parts of the exploiting classes will view national liberation and state-led development as a means to fulfill their interests, and so will support the party as it leads these efforts. Yet today's global economy works very differently than it did when this idea was formulated. Former colonial zones are now formally independent, so that elites in underdeveloped countries are no longer politically dominated by outside powers. Capital expands not through the protectionist trade monopolies of imperialist states but through financial flows and extended commodity production chains. In this context, the bourgeoisies of underdeveloped countries stand to benefit by integrating as "junior partners" in global capital—as have the "Asian Tigers" and the BRICS nations (Brazil, Russia, India, China, and South Africa)—rather than pursuing protectionist state development.

The effect of these new conditions on New Democratic strategy has been illustrated in Nepal by the fate of the United Communist Party of Nepal (Maoist). After toppling the Nepalese monarchy in 2006 in alliance with other political parties, the UCPN(M) found foreign investors more than willing to subcontract with domestic industry in exchange for the establishment of Special Economic Zones and strike bans.[32] No longer limited to coddling domestic firms under New Democracy to achieve capital formation, the party leadership readily embraced these policies. Mao's categories, developed in an earlier period, no longer applied to the conditions at hand. To avoid these pitfalls, today's revolutionaries must subject Mao's notion of New Democracy to the test of contemporary material conditions, along with the Marxist-Leninist concepts—semi-colonial nation, transitional stage, state capitalism, and so on—upon which it is premised.

Class struggle under socialism: The notion of "class struggle under socialism" broadly refers to Mao's notion of socialist transition developed in the 1950s and 1960s. While asserting the chaotic nature of revolutionary transition, the concept nonetheless obscures the exploitative class relations of state capitalist societies and thus misconstrues what "class struggle" under socialist regimes actually consists of. Mao assumes nationalized industry and the dictatorship of the party guarantees the transition from socialism to communism. He thus conceives of "class struggle under socialism" as a limited battle against reactionary ideology, corrupt officials, and not-yet-nationalized property forms, while defending state capitalist production and the party's position in power.

As a result, Mao's notion amounts to a kind of state capitalist reformism, couched in Marxist language. Furthermore, it obscures crucial questions of revolutionary transition that go beyond state capitalism: how to transform relations of production and develop pockets of directly communist production and distribution? How to enlarge these spheres while destroying capitalist relations and social formations? How to guarantee communist social reproduction by producing its preconditions in the course of this struggle? To grapple with these questions on a concrete level, militants must jettison the Maoist notion of socialist transition as such.

Two-line struggle: Mao developed the notion of "two-line struggle" to describe how bourgeois perspectives arose within the CCP after the revolution. For Mao, the residual ideas of capitalist society, and vested interest groups in the party, were the sources of this dynamic; he refused to recognize how the party's position at the head of state capitalist exploitation conditioned shifts in consciousness. Thus Mao's concept is essentially detached from any grounding in material social relations. As a result, the Maoist tradition tends to take two-line struggle as simply a universal feature of all revolutionary organizations under capitalism, of whatever size, in state power or outside it.

In some cases, Maoist militants use the phrase to reiterate the truism that politics involves debates between differing perspectives. Yet Mao's concept also distorts the manner in which this debate is understood. Often two-line struggle in Maoist organizations reduces political positions to two opposed sides under platitudes such as "rightist deviation" and "leftist deviation," thus greatly obscuring their content, premises, and nuance. In other cases, it requires exposing opposed positions as not only incorrect but also reactionary and "bourgeois," in the sense of "the bourgeoisie within the party." Debates thus tend toward oversimplification, hyperbole, and denunciation. Instead of using Mao's concept as a guide to political debate, militants today could best reinterpret two-line struggle as a description of how Marxist politics becomes bourgeois ideology, in revolutionary organizations that become managers and administrators of capitalist exploitation.

Women hold up half the sky: The gender politics adopted by Mao and the CCP largely replicate the positions of the Second International and orthodox Marxism-Leninism. Most CCP leaders believed women's liberation would be achieved through participation in wage labor, a view that comfortably paralleled the party's state capitalist development strategy and cast autonomous women's struggles as unnecessary disruptions to production. Young women mobilized within the confines of these politics during the GLF and the CR, embracing masculine forms of political expression outside of their homes and villages. But these efforts did not challenge the gendered division of labor or alter the party's gender politics. The Maoist tradition offers little to revolutionaries who seek the liberation of women and queer and trans people. Today's militants can best pursue these goals by drawing upon autonomist feminist politics that critique the division between production and reproduction and aim at the abolition of gender and the family.

Politics in command: Developed to guide cadres in mass work while overseeing capital accumulation, Mao's notion of "putting politics in command" instructed party members to mobilize workers and peasants based on political slogans and "non-material incentives," rather than on wages and material gains. This slogan was used in the labor mobilizations of the GLF, and the crackdown on the "wind of economism" during the CR, to obscure the class interests of the proletariat and peasantry and their conflict with the party. Today, Maoist militants often interpret "politics in command" to mean emphasizing broad revolutionary goals over "economistic" demands. They thereby blur Mao's concept with Lenin's notion, from *What Is to Be Done?*, of bringing political consciousness to economic battles from the outside.

As a general call to offer revolutionary perspectives to everyday struggles, the notion of putting politics in command is useful and parallels other conceptions from the anarchist and communist traditions. But Mao's lack of attention to class interest shapes the manner in which his notion is applied. For many Maoist groups, putting politics in command simply entails exhorting people to pursue the organization's chosen program, or declaring what goals proletarians "must" take up out of moral commitment. In common with many Leninist interpretations of vanguard leadership, these methods assume the validity of the party's political line, and obscure proletarian self-activity. To correct these blind spots, revolutionaries today must develop a praxis that seeks out revolutionary horizons present within the proletariat's own contradictory thought and action.

For revolutionaries who aim at a free anarchist and communist society, Maoism as a whole must be rejected. It may be possible to extract particular strategic concepts, work methods, or slogans from the Chinese experience, after subjecting them to a rigorous critique. But these elements must then be embedded in a set of revolutionary politics far different from those developed by Mao from the 1920s to the 1970s.

A revolutionary movement today must place contributing to revolution on a world scale over and above the consolidation of a new social system in any individual state. The spread of global production chains makes any attempt to create a revolutionary society within the bounds of a single state increasingly incoherent. Submerged in a capitalist world market, and intimately reliant on commodity production from all corners of the globe, no state will be able to develop a qualitatively new society within its borders alone, and attempts to do so will either assume a capitalist form or descend into authoritarian autarky. Today's revolutionaries must certainly work to maintain and expand rebel territories that allow for revolutionary activity, on whatever scale. But we must also cast aside the illusion of building "socialism" within these enclaves and maintain unwavering and critical analysis of the relations of production operating within them. Our strategy should begin on the level of trade blocs and hemispheres.

A revolutionary organization today must develop work methods that recognize, grapple with, and galvanize the self-activity of the proletariat. This requires analyzing mass consciousness as a contradictory interpretation of reality with real effects and potentials, from which revolutionaries stand to learn even as they contribute to it. This perspective stands fundamentally opposed to party substitutionism and Stalinist dialectics. While revolutionary groups draw on the history of class struggle and employ particular theories and methods in their work, they are but one locus in which the experience, lessons, and consciousness of the exploited are crystallized and sustained. Potentially revolutionary consciousness is also carried in everyday "good sense," traditional community organizations, and subcultures outside the established left, and it is not reducible to any one revolutionary organization. Revolutionaries must therefore develop a praxis that allows them to contribute the ideas, methods, and historical lessons they carry to mass struggles, while still seeking out and building upon the self-activity of the oppressed and exploited, which alone prefigures a new society.

Today's revolutionary movements may find themselves waging struggles with the sanction of sympathetic leaders in positions of state power, whether socialist, nationalist, or otherwise. Such situations are unavoidable, and taking advantage of them is strategically necessary, but revolutionaries must always clearly identify the class allies and class enemies of proletarian mass organizations. They must also develop the capacity of these organizations to operate autonomously from bourgeois power, defend this capacity, and prepare proletarians for the overthrow of the state itself. To abdicate this task is to stunt the development of independent theory and organization among mass movements, and ensure they will be unprepared when their "friends" in state power turn on them.

Today as in the past, a revolutionary movement must pursue a world in which everyone enjoys control over the means of production and free access to the means of subsistence. This society cannot be brought into existence simply by transferring legal ownership of capitalist enterprises to a ruling party or state, which then purports to represent the interests of the proletariat through its political line. Such arrangements preserve capitalist relations of exploitation, thus generating daily and hourly the capitalist relations and standards of value that strangle revolutionary social transformation. A far-reaching transformation the social relationships through which we produce and reproduce human and non-human life, day after day, can be the only goal of revolutionaries, and the standard by which we judge revolutions.

Finally, today's revolutionary movements must prepare for the challenges that follow on the heels every revolutionary rupture. As has been the case in every modern revolution, a new society in emergence will be forced to defend itself from internal enemies among the overthrown classes, external enemies and hostile states, and from the ideological detritus of capitalist society. However, the methods used to address these problems must not contribute to the reproduction of class relations. Instead they must defend and deepen the communist social relations struggling to reproduce themselves on expanded scales, and actively undermine capitalist relations in the process. To the extent that capitalist relations of production still exist in a given social formation, the presence of a specialized repressive apparatus is a sufficient condition for their reproduction. Revolutionaries must oppose the establishment of a state that will direct and reproduce exploitation, and instead encourage forms of mass, federated, armed, and directly democratic social organization. There is no alternative to the anarchist thesis: the state must be smashed.

This path offers as many questions as it does answers. But the strengths, weaknesses, challenges, and failures of past revolutions help us to illuminate the contours of a possible future society. By critically evaluating these experiences, we can guess at what awaits us in the darkness ahead. This task is replete with ambiguities and questions. If we are to avoid repeating the needless sacrifices of the twentieth century—those of Maoism included—we have no choice but to pursue it.

■ FURTHER READING

General Histories

Andors, Phyllis. *The Unfinished Liberation of Chinese Women: 1949–1980*. Bloomington: Indiana University Press, 1983.

Bailey, Paul J. *Women and Gender in Twentieth-Century China*. New York: Palgrave Macmillan, 2012.

Bianco, Lucien. *Origins of the Chinese Revolution*. Stanford: Stanford University Press, 1971.

Chesneaux, Jean. *China from 1911 to Liberation*. New York: Pantheon, 1977.

Chesneaux, Jean. *China: The People's Republic, 1949–1976*. New York: Pantheon, 1979.

Dirlik, Arif. *The Origins of Chinese Communism*. New York: Oxford University Press, 1989.

MacFarquhar, Roderick. *The Origins of the Cultural Revolution*, vols. 1–3. New York: Columbia University Press.

Meisner, Maurice. *Mao's China and After: A History of the People's Republic*. New York: Free Press, 1986.

Potter, Sulamith Heins, and Jack M. Potter, *China's Peasants: The Anthropology of a Revolution*. Cambridge: Cambridge University Press, 1990.

Selden, Mark. *The Political Economy of Chinese Development*. Armonk, NY: M.E. Sharpe, 1993.

Sheehan, Jackie. *Chinese Workers: A New History*. New York: Routledge, 1998.

Stacey, Judith. *Patriarchy and Socialist Revolution in China*. Berkeley: University of California Press, 1983.

Whyte, Martin King, and William L. Parish, *Urban Life in Contemporary China*. Chicago: University of Chicago Press, 1984.

Particular Histories

Andreas, Joel. *Rise of the Red Engineers: The Cultural Revolution and the Origins of China's New Class*. Stanford: Stanford University Press, 2009.

Apter, David, and Tony Saich, *Revolutionary Discourse in Mao's Republic.* Cambridge, MA: Harvard University Press, 1994.

Bernardo, Joao. "Social Struggles in China." Revolt Against Plenty, http://www.revoltagainstplenty.com/index.php/recent/198-joao-bernardo.html.

Bettelheim, Charles. *Cultural Revolution and Industrial Organization in China.* New York: Monthly Review Press, 1974.

Harrison, James P. *The Long March to Power: A History of the Chinese Communist Party, 1921–72.* New York: Praeger, 1972.

Hinton, William. *Fanshen.* New York: Monthly Review Press, 1969.

Howe, Christopher. *China's Economy: A Basic Guide.* New York: Basic, 1978.

Isaacs, Harold. *The Tragedy of the Chinese Revolution.* London: Secker & Warburg, 1938. Note: 1938 edition only.

Leys, Simon. *The Chairman's New Clothes.* New York: St. Martin's Press, 1977.

MacFarquhar, Roderick. *The Hundred Flowers Campaign and the Chinese Intellectuals.* New York: Praeger, 1960.

Maitan, Livio. *Party, Army, and Masses in China.* Atlantic Highlands, NJ: Humanities Press, 1976.

Pantsov, Alexander. *The Bolsheviks and the Chinese Revolution 1919–1927.* Honolulu: University of Hawai'i Press, 2000.

Perry, Elizabeth. "Shanghai's Strike Wave of 1957." *China Quarterly* 137 (1994).

Perry, Elizabeth, and Li Xun, *Proletarian Power: Shanghai in the Cultural Revolution.* Boulder: Westview Press, 1997.

Selden, Mark. *The Yenan Way in Revolutionary China.* Cambridge, MA: Harvard University Press, 1971.

70s collective, eds. *China: The Revolution Is Dead, Long Live the Revolution!* Montreal: Black Rose Books, 1977.

Unger, Jonathan. "Whither China? Yang Xiguang, Red Capitalists, and the Social Turmoil of the Cultural Revolution." *Modern China* 17, no. 1 (1991).

Wang, Shaoguang. "'New Trends of Thought' on the Cultural Revolution." *Journal of Contemporary China* 21, no. 8 (1999).

Wu, Yiching. *Revolution at the Margins: Social Protest and Politics of Class in China, 1966–69.* Cambridge, MA: Harvard University Press, 2014.

Yang, Jisheng, *Tombstone: The Great Chinese Famine, 1958–1962.* New York: Farrar, Straus and Giroux, 2012.

Theoretical and Philosophical

Aufheben, "What Was the USSR?" parts I–IV, *Aufheben* 6–9 (1997–2000).

Chattopadhyay, Paresh. *The Marxian Concept of Capital and the Soviet Experience.* Westport, CT: Praeger, 1994.

Glaberman, Marty. "Mao as Dialectician," *International Philosophical Quarterly* 8 (1968).

James, C.L.R. *Notes on Dialectics: Hegel, Marx, Lenin.* Westport, CT: Lawrence Hill, 1980.

James, C.L.R., Raya Dunayevskaya, and Grace Lee Boggs, *State Capitalism and World Revolution.* Oakland: PM Press, 2013.

Knight, Nick. *Mao Zedong on Dialectical Materialism.* Armonk, NY: M.E. Sharpe, 1990.

Ollman, Bertell. *Dance of the Dialectic: Steps in Marx's Method.* Urbana: University of Illinois, 2003.

Sheehan, Helena. *Marxism and the Philosophy of Science: A Critical History.* Atlantic Highlands, NJ: Humanities Press, 1985.

van der Linden, Marcel. *Western Marxism and the Soviet Union.* Boston: Brill, 2007.

Young, Graham. "Mao Zedong and Class Struggle in Socialist Society." *The Australian Journal of Chinese Affairs* 16 (1986).

Mao Texts

Analysis of the Classes in Chinese Society, March 1926.
Report on an Investigation of the Peasant Movement In Hunan, March 1927.
On Practice, July 1937.
On Contradiction, August 1937.
Dialectical Materialism (Lecture Notes), 1937.
The Chinese Revolution and the Chinese Communist Party, December 1939.
On New Democracy, January 1940.
On the People's Democratic Dictatorship, June 1949.
On the Ten Major Relationships, April 1956.
On the Correct Handling of Contradictions Among the People, February 1957.
Reading Notes on the Soviet Text 'Political Economy,' 1961–1962.

Military Writings

Why Is It That Red Political Power Can Exist in China?, October 1928.
The Struggle in the Chingkiang Mountains, November 1928
Problems of Strategy in China's Revolutionary War, December 1936.
On Guerilla Warfare, 1937.
Basic Tactics, 1937.
Problems of Strategy in Guerrilla in War Against Japan, May 1938.
On Protracted War, May 1938.

CCP Texts

On the Historical Experience of the Dictatorship of the Proletariat, 1959.

The Polemic of the General Line of the International Communist Movement, 1964.

Decision of the Central Committee of the Chinese Communist Party Concerning the Great Proletarian Cultural Revolution (Sixteen Points), August 1966.

Raymond Lotta, ed., *Maoist Economics & the Revolutionary Road to Communism: The Shanghai Textbook*, 1974.

Zhang Chunqiao, *On Exercising All-Round Dictatorship Over the Bourgeoisie*, 1974.

Yao Wenyuan, *On the Social Basis of the Lin Piao Antiparty Clique*, 1975.

■ NOTES

Introduction

1. Loren Goldner, "Notes Toward a Critique of Maoism," http://breaktheirhaughtypower.org/notes-towards-a-critique-of-maoism.

I. Prologue: The First Chinese Revolution

1. Lucien Bianco, *Origins of the Chinese Revolution* (Stanford: Stanford University Press, 1971), 54.
2. Ibid., 92–93.
3. Kay Ann Johnson, *Women, the Family, and Peasant Revolution in China* (Chicago: University of Chicago Press, 1983), 30.
4. See Eric Wolf, *Peasant Wars of the Twentieth Century* (New York: Harper & Row, 1969), chap. 3.
5. Harold Isaacs, *The Tragedy of the Chinese Revolution* (London: Secker & Warburg, 1938), chap. 3. Also see Alexander Pantsov, *The Bolsheviks and the Chinese Revolution 1919–1927*, and Arif Dirlik, *The Origins of Chinese Communism* and *Anarchism in the Chinese Revolution* for an overview of this period.
6. For an account of these years, see Simon Pirani's *The Russian Revolution in Retreat: 1920–1924* (New York: Routledge, 2008) and G.P. Maximoff's *The Guillotine at Work*, vols. 1 and 2.
7. For a sweeping history of these developments, see Raya Dunayevskaya, *Marxism and Freedom from 1776 until Today* (New York: Bookman Associates, 1958). For a parallel critical history of the social democratic tradition, see Endnotes, "A History of Separation," http://endnotes.org.uk/en/endnotes-a-history-of-separation.
8. The proper relationship between the communist party and the national bourgeoisie in anticolonial struggles remained a topic of intense debate within the Comintern, however. For an account of the failure of 1927 from dissident Comintern perspectives, see Leon Trotsky, *Problems of the Chinese Revolution* (New York: Pioneer, 1932), and M.N. Roy, *Revolution and Counter-Revolution in China* (Calcutta: Renaissance Publishers, 1946).

9. Bianco, *Origins*, 54–56.
10. Isaacs, *Tragedy*, chap. 10.
11. Ibid., chaps. 11–12.
12. Ibid., chap. 17. See Maurice Meisner's *Mao's China and After*, chap. 3, for an overview of this period.
13. Jane Degras, *The Communist International: 1919–1943, Documents*, vol. 2 (London: Oxford University Press, 1956), 529.
14. Isaacs, *Tragedy*, chap. 18.
15. Bianco, *Origins*, 64–70.

II. People's War from the Countryside

1. Michael Sheng, "Mao, Stalin, and the Formation of the Anti-Japanese United Front: 1935–37," *China Quarterly* 129 (1992): 149–70.
2. Lucien Bianco, *Origins of the Chinese Revolution* (Stanford: Stanford University Press, 1971), 68.
3. James Harrison, *The Long March to Power: A History of the Chinese Communist Party, 1921–72* (New York: Praeger, 1972), 319–21.
4. Ibid., 271.
5. Ibid., 311–13.
6. For an overview of this period, see William Hinton, *Fanshen: A Documentary of Revolution in a Chinese Village* (New York: Monthly Review Press, 1969), and Mark Selden, *The Yenan Way in Revolutionary China* (Cambridge, MA: Harvard University Press, 1971).
7. Mao, "Current Problems of Tactics in the Anti-Japanese United Front," March 1940, https://www.marxists.org/reference/archive/mao/selected-works/volume-2/mswv2_34.htm.
8. Bill Brugger, *China: Liberation and Transformation, 1942–1962* (London: Croom Helm, 1981), 36.
9. Mao, "Some Questions Concerning Methods of Leadership," June 1943, https://www.marxists.org/reference/archive/mao/selected-works/volume-3/mswv3_13.htm.
10. For an example of an attempt to overcome these shortcomings within a Maoist framework, see *The Mass Line and the American Revolutionary Movement* by Scott Harrison, available at http://www.massline.info.
11. Kay Ann Johnson, *Women, the Family, and Peasant Revolution in China* (Chicago: University of Chicago Press, 1983), 67–68.
12. See Ting Ling, "Thoughts on 8 March (Women's Day)," 1942, https://libcom.org/library/thoughts-8-march-women%E2%80%99s-day.
13. Johnson, *Women*, 73–74.
14. Paul Bailey, *Women and Gender in Twentieth-Century China* (New York: Palgrave Macmillan, 2012), 98.
15. For an overview of this perspective, see Selma James, *Sex, Race, and Class—The Perspective of Winning* (Oakland: PM Press, 2012); Silvia Federici, *Revolution at Point Zero* (Oakland: PM Press, 2012); Lise Vogel,

Marxism and the Oppression of Women (Leiden: Brill, 2013); and Endnotes, "The Logic of Gender," *Endnotes* 3 (2013), http://https://endnotes.org.uk/en/endnotes-the-logic-of-gender.

16. For an overview of the party's gender politics in the Yenan period, see Judith Stacey, *Patriarchy and Socialist Revolution in China* (Berkeley: University of California Press, 1983).

17. Harrison, *Long March to Power*, 458.

18. See "Theses on the United Front" adopted by the Executive Committee of the Comintern, December 1921, https://www.marxists.org/history/international/comintern/4th-congress/united-front.htm.

19. Michael Sheng, "Mao, Stalin, and the Formation of the Anti-Japanese United Front: 1935–37," *China Quarterly* 129 (March 1992): 167–69.

20. See Mao, "On the Question of Political Power in the Anti-Japanese Base Areas," March 1940, https://www.marxists.org/reference/archive/mao/selected-works/volume-2/mswv2_33.htm.

21. Harrison, *Long March to Power*, 318.

22. Mark Selden, *The Yenan Way in Revolutionary China* (Cambridge, MA: Harvard University Press, 1971), 98–99.

23. See "Decision of the CC on land policy in the anti-Japanese base areas," January 1942, in Conrad Brandt, Benjamin Schwartz, and John Fairbank, eds., *A Documentary History of Chinese Communism* (New York: Athenaeum, 1973), 276–85.

24. See Mao, "The Chinese Revolution and the Chinese Communist Party," December 1939, https://www.marxists.org/reference/archive/mao/selected-works/volume-2/mswv2_23.htm.

25. See Mao, "On New Democracy," January 1940, https://www.marxists.org/reference/archive/mao/selected-works/volume-2/mswv2_26.htm.

26. See Mao, "Current Problems of Tactics in the Anti-Japanese United Front," March 1940; "On the Question of Political Power in the Anti-Japanese Base Areas," March 1940; "On Some Important Problems of the Party's Present Policy," January 1948; and "On the Policy Concerning Industry and Commerce," February 1948, all on Marxists.org.

27. Mao, "The Only Road for the Transformation of Capitalist Industry and Commerce," September 1953. Also Mao, "On State Capitalism," July 1953, https://www.marxists.org/reference/archive/mao/selected-works/volume-5/mswv5_30.htm.

28. Nick Knight, *Mao Zedong on Dialectical Materialism: Writings on Philosophy, 1937* (Armonk, NY: M.E. Sharpe, 1990), 32–38.

29. For an overview of debates in this period, see Helena Sheehan, *Marxism and the Philosophy of Science* (Atlantic Highlands, NJ: Humanities Press, 1985), chaps. 4 and 5.

30. Knight, *Dialectical Materialism*, 33.

31. Ibid., 89.

32. Ibid., 103.

33. Ibid., 115.

34. See Anton Pannekoek, *Lenin as Philosopher* (New York: Merlin Press, 1975), chaps. 2 and 7. Interestingly, the tendency toward vulgar materialism that Pannekoek highlights is also present in Bakunin's philosophical work. Bakunin too reduces consciousness to a property of the brain, and ultimately to a "reproduction in the mind and brain" of outside physical matter, its "mediated pattern." However, he also draws a distinction between "universal laws" governing all matter, and "particular laws" which only govern specific orders of phenomena, such as laws of social development. Thus Bakunin admits the possibility that social and mental phenomena may be guided by their own irreducible dynamics. See G.P. Maximoff, *The Political Philosophy of Bakunin* (New York: Free Press, 1953), chaps. 1 and 2.

35. See C.L.R. James, *Notes on Dialectics: Hegel, Marx, Lenin* (Westport, CT: Lawrence Hill, 1980), 16–33.

36. This shortcoming was noted by the Marxist-Leninist Education Project in 1980, as *On Practice* was becoming standard reading among left groups in the New Communist Movement. See Marxist-Leninist Education Project Theory of Knowledge Group, "Dialectical or Mechanical Materialism (A Response)," *Line of March* 1 (1980), https://www.marxists.org/history/erol/ncm-6/lom-reply-newlin.htm.

37. Today many Maoists claim Mao rejected the entire notion of the "negation of the negation," an ultimate negation which brings a contradiction to an end in a final synthesis. This isn't entirely accurate. While Mao insisted that "there is no such thing as the negation of the negation" in 1964—see Knight, *Dialectical Materialism*, page 18—the term is present in his *Lecture Notes* and was used in speeches throughout the 1950s. It appears the term gradually fell out of favor without clear philosophical exposition as to its strengths or weaknesses.

38. For a useful overview of Marx's conception, see Bertell Ollman, *Dance of the Dialectic: Steps in Marx's Method* (Urbana: University of Illinois, 2003).

39. See Martin Glaberman, "Mao as Dialectician," *International Philosophical Quarterly* 8 (1968).

40. This is a common critique of the Marxist tradition as a whole. See Tabor, *The Tyranny of Theory: A Contribution to the Critique of Marxism* (Albert: Black Cat Press, 2013) and Cornelius Castoriadis, *The Imaginary Institution of Society* (Cambridge, MA: MIT Press, 1998).

41. Modern military theory distinguishes between several levels of strategy and tactics, from the "grand strategy" of statecraft and geopolitics, to specifically military strategy, to "battle doctrine" employed in specific operational theaters, to tactics employed in particular engagements. Though Mao did not use these exact categories, his military writings broadly cover the last three categories.

42. Mao, "On Protracted War," secs. 10–11, https://www.marxists.org/reference/archive/mao/selected-works/volume-2/mswv2_09.htm. Also see

Mao, *On Guerrilla Warfare*, chap. 4, https://www.marxists.org/reference/archive/mao/works/1937/guerrilla-warfare/.

43. Mao, "On Protracted War," secs. 32–33.
44. Ibid., secs. 35–38.
45. Mao, *On Guerrilla Warfare*, chap 5.
46. See Mao, "Basic Tactics," and Mao, *On Guerrilla Warfare*, chaps. 5 and 7.
47. Mao, *On Guerrilla Warfare*, chap. 1.
48. Mao, *Problems of Strategy in Guerrilla War Against Japan*, chap. 8, https://www.marxists.org/reference/archive/mao/selected-works/volume-2/mswv2_08.htm.
49. Mao, "On Protracted War," secs. 73–76.
50. Strangely, Mao anticipates that the world-scale encirclement of World War II will culminate in global revolution and world peace: "We can foresee that the result of this war will not be the salvation of capitalism, but its approach to collapse. . . . Once man has eliminated capitalism, he will reach the age of permanent peace, and will never again desire war. Neither armies, nor warships, nor military planes, nor poison gas will then be needed. Thereafter man will never know war again. The revolutionary war which has already begun is part of the war for permanent peace." See Mao, "On Protracted War," sec. 57.
51. *Weich'i* is known as *go* in Japan. See Mao, *Problems of Strategy in Guerrilla War Against Japan*, chap. 6, sec. 5, and Mao, "On Protracted War," secs. 52–54.
52. Mao, "On Protracted War," sec. 60.
53. Ibid., 62.
54. Ibid., 67.
55. Mao Zedong, "The Role of Chinese Communist Party in the National War," in *Mao Tse-tung: Selected Works*, vol. 2 (New York: International Publishers, 1954), 250.
56. Mao, *Problems of Strategy in Guerrilla War Against Japan*, chap. 6, sec. 3.
57. Mao, *On Guerilla Warfare*, chap. 6.
58. Ibid.
59. Mao, *Problems of Strategy in Guerrilla War Against Japan*, chap. 6, sec. 3.
60. Mao, "On Protracted War," secs. 112–17.
61. Mao, "Basic Tactics," chap. 15, secs. 5–10.
62. Mao, "On Correcting Mistaken Ideas in the Party," sec. 2, December 1929, https://www.marxists.org/reference/archive/mao/selected-works/volume-1/mswv1_5.htm.
63. Mao, *On Guerilla Warfare*, Appendix.
64. See Mao, "Turn the Army into a Working Force," February 1949, https://www.marxists.org/reference/archive/mao/selected-works/volume-4/mswv4_54.htm, and "Make Our Army a Great School of Mao Tse-tung's Thought," 1966, https://www.marxists.org/subject/china/peking-review/1966/PR1966-32f.htm.

65. Harrison, *Long March to Power*, 316.
66. Selden, *The Yenan Way*, 177–79.
67. David Apter and Tony Saich, *Revolutionary Discourse in Mao's Republic* (Cambridge, MA: Harvard University Press, 1994).
68. Lucien Bianco, *Origins of the Chinese Revolution* (Stanford: Stanford University Press, 1971), 150.
69. Ibid., 155–56.
70. Mao, *On Guerilla Warfare*, chap. 6.
71. See Mao, "On Some Important Problems of the Party's Present Policies," January 1948, https://www.marxists.org/reference/archive/mao/selected-works/volume-4/mswv4_26.htm.
72. See Mao, "On the Policy Concerning Industry and Commerce," February 1948.
73. Jean Chesneaux, *China: The People's Republic, 1949–1979* (New York: Pantheon: 1979), 10.
74. Ibid., 4.

III. The CCP in State Power

1. Nai-Ruenn Chen and Walter Galenson, *The Chinese Economy Under Communism* (Chicago: Aldine, 1969), 51–53.
2. Ibid., 33.
3. Elizabeth Perry, "Shanghai's Strike Wave of 1957," *China Quarterly* 137 (1994): 8–9.
4. See T.J. Hughes and Evan Luard, *The Economic Development of Communist China, 1949–1960* (Oxford: Oxford University Press, 1961), chap. 13.
5. Kay Ann Johnson, *Women, the Family, and Peasant Revolution in China* (Chicago: University of Chicago Press, 1983), chaps. 9–10.
6. Wang Zheng, "Dilemmas of Inside Agitators: Chinese State Feminists in 1957," in *The History of the PRC (1949–1976)*, ed. Julia Strauss (Cambridge: Cambridge University Press, 2007).
7. Jean Chesneaux, *China: The People's Republic, 1949–1979* (New York: Pantheon, 1979), 59–60.
8. Ibid., 46–47.
9. Jackie Sheehan, *Chinese Workers: A New History* (New York: Routledge, 1998), 62.
10. Phyllis Andors, *The Unfinished Liberation of Chinese Women: 1949–1980* (Bloomington: Indiana University Press, 1983), 93.
11. Charles Hoffman, *Work Incentive Practices and Policies in the People's Republic of China, 1953–1965* (Albany: SUNY Press 1967), 45–53. See also Christopher Howe, *China's Economy: A Basic Guide* (New York: Basic Books, 1978), 47–51.
12. Hoffman, *Work Incentive Practices*, 84–85.
13. Howe, *China's Economy*, chap. 6.
14. Elizabeth Perry, "Shanghai's Strike Wave of 1957," *China Quarterly* 137 (1994): 8.

15. Victor Lippit, *The Economic Development of China* (Armonk, NY: M.E. Sharpe, 1987), 149–50.

16. Jackie Sheehan, *Chinese Workers: A New History* (New York: Routledge, 1998), 57–60.

17. Ibid., 32.

18. Ibid., 75.

19. Howe, *China's Economy*, 19.

20. Mark Selden, *The Political Economy of Chinese Development* (Armonk, NY: M.E. Sharpe, 1993), 170–71. See also Robert Ash, "Squeezing the Peasants: Gain Extraction, Food Consumption and Rural Living Standards in Mao's China," in *The History of the PRC (1949–1976)*, ed. Julia Strauss (Cambridge: Cambridge University Press, 2002).

21. Ezra F. Vogel, "From Revolutionary to Semi-Bureaucrat: The 'Regularization' of Cadres," *China Quarterly* 29 (1967): 36–40.

22. Lowell Dittmer, *China's Continuous Revolution: The Post-Liberation Epoch, 1949–1981* (Berkeley: University of California Press, 1989), 60.

23. Roderick MacFarquhar, *The Origins of the Cultural Revolution, Vol. 1: Contradictions among the People, 1956–1957* (New York: Columbia University Press, 1974), 365–66.

24. Ibid., 171. See also Lorenz Luthi, *The Sino-Soviet Split: Cold War in the Communist World* (Princeton: Princeton University Press, 2008), chap. 2.

25. This figure includes deaths from the 1951 land reforms and the concurrent Campaign to Suppress Counter-Revolutionaries. See Julia Strauss, "Morality, Coercion and State Building by Campaign in the Early PRC," in *The History of the PRC (1949–1976)*, ed. Julia Strauss (Cambridge: Cambridge University Press, 2002).

26. See Peng Shuzi, "Two Interviews on the 'Cultural Revolution,'" *World Outlook* (1967), https://www.marxists.org/archive/peng/1967/interviews.htm.

27. Roderick MacFarquhar, *The Hundred Flowers Campaign and Chinese Intellectuals* (New York: Praeger, 1960), 141.

28. Elizabeth Perry, "Shanghai's Strike Wave of 1957," *China Quarterly* 137 (1994): 1–5.

29. T.J. Hughes and Evan Luard, *The Economic Development of Communist China, 1949–1960* (Oxford: Oxford University Press, 1961), 122.

30. Jackie Sheehan, *Chinese Workers*, 48.

31. Perry, "Shanghai's Strike Wave," 1–5.

32. Hughes and Luard, *Economic Development*, 159.

33. Wang Zheng, "Dilemmas of Inside Agitators: Chinese State Feminists in 1957," in *The History of the PRC (1949–1976)*, ed. Julia Strauss (Cambridge: Cambridge University Press, 2007).

34. Hughes and Luard, *Economic Development*, 123–24.

35. Stephen Andors, *China's Industrial Revolution: Politics, Planning, and Management, 1949 to the Present* (New York: Pantheon, 1977), 79–87.

36. Mark Selden, *The Political Economy of Chinese Development* (Armonk, NY: M.E. Sharpe, 1993), 83.

37. Victor Lippit, *The Economic Development of China* (Armonk, NY: M.E. Sharpe, 1987), 111.

38. Jean Chesneaux, *China: The People's Republic, 1949–1979* (New York: Pantheon, 1979), 88.

39. Yang Jisheng, *Tombstone: The Great Chinese Famine, 1958–1962* (New York: Farrar, Straus and Giroux, 2012), 177.

40. Charles Hoffman, *Work Incentive Practices and Policies in the People's Republic of China, 1953–1965* (Albany: SUNY Press, 1967), 73–74.

41. See Simon Pirani, *The Russian Revolution in Retreat, 1920–24: Soviet Workers and the New Communist Elite* (New York: Routledge, 2008), 141–55.

42. Jisheng, *Tombstone*, 299.

43. Kay Ann Johnson, *Women, the Family, and Peasant Revolution in China* (Chicago: University of Chicago Press, 1983), 160–69. For an overview of this dynamic in Third World cases, see Maria Mies, *Patriarchy and Accumulation on a World Scale* (London: Zed, 1998), chap. 6.

44. Chesneaux, *China*, 102.

45. Andors, *The Unfinished Liberation of Chinese Women*, 50.

46. Bill Brugger, *China: Liberation and Transformation, 1942–1962* (London: Croom Helm, 1981), 192.

47. Roderick MacFarquhar, *The Origins of the Cultural Revolution, Vol. 2: The Great Leap Forward, 1958–1960* (New York: Columbia University Press, 1983), 85.

48. See Jisheng, *Tombstone*, chap. 7.

49. Ibid., 262.

50. Ibid., 253.

51. Chesneaux, *China*, 102.

52. Jisheng, *Tombstone*, 42.

53. Ibid., chap. 1.

54. See Mao, "Speech at the Lushan conference," https://www.marxists.org/reference/archive/mao/selected-works/volume-8/mswv8_34.htm. For a comprehensive account of the party debates surrounding the GLF, see Luthi, *The Sino-Soviet Split*, chap. 4; and MacFarquhar, *The Origins of the Cultural Revolution, Vol. 2*.

55. Jisheng, *Tombstone*, 453–56.

56. Ibid., 457.

57. Ibid., 450.

58. Ibid., 335.

59. Ibid., 185.

60. Ibid., 473–74.

61. For an evaluation of the different estimates and the methods used to arrive at them, see Jisheng, *Tombstone*, chap. 11.

62. In both cases, attempted developmental leaps cost around 5–6 percent of the population.

63. MacFarquhar, *Origins, Vol. 2*, 326–27.

64. Ibid., 330.

65. For a good visual representation of the impact of the GLF, see the *China Statistical Yearbook, 1997* (Beijing: 1997), 41. Per capita production indices for ten main agricultural commodities all show a dramatic drop by 1962, many to below 1951 levels. Most indices do not even return to 1957 levels until 1965.

66. For a full account of Sino-Soviet tensions in this period, see Luthi, *The Sino-Soviet Split*.

67. Mao, "Reading Notes on the Soviet Text *Political Economy*," 1961–1962, note 39, https://www.marxists.org/reference/archive/mao/selected-works/volume-8/mswv8_64.htm.

68. Ibid., notes 40, 42.

69. Ibid., note 21.

70. Ibid., note 8.

71. Ibid., note 30.

72. Ibid., note 29.

73. Ibid., note 66.

74. Ibid., note 45.

75. Ibid., note 25.

76. Ibid., note 43.

77. Ibid., note 19.

78. Ibid., note 32.

79. Ibid., note 57.

80. Ibid., 24.

IV. The Cultural Revolution

1. Christopher Howe, *China's Economy: A Basic Guide* (New York: Basic Books, 1978), 23.

2. Ibid., 24–25.

3. Yiching Wu, *The Cultural Revolution at the Margins: Chinese Socialism in Crisis* (Cambridge, MA: Harvard University Press, 2014), 25.

4. Mark Selden, *The Political Economy of Chinese Development* (Armonk, NY: M.E. Sharpe, 1992), 174.

5. Howe, *China's Economy*, 23.

6. For an analysis that locates stagnating class mobility prior to the Cultural Revolution in the context of the maturation of Chinese state capitalism, see Joao Bernardo, *Social Struggles in China*, http://www.revoltagainstplenty.com/index.php/recent/198-joao-bernardo.html.

7. *Ra Hui Dismissed from Office* was written by Wu Han, a scholar and then deputy mayor of Beijing. As the CR set in, Wu Han was jailed, committing suicide in prison in 1969.

8. See "Circular of the Central Committee of the Communist Party of China on the Great Proletarian Cultural Revolution," May 1966, https://www.marxists.org/subject/china/documents/cpc/cc_gpcr.htm.

9. Joel Andreas, *Rise of the Red Engineers: The Cultural Revolution and the Origins of China's New Class* (Stanford: Stanford University Press, 2009), 97.

10. See "Decision of the Central Committee of the Chinese Communist Party Concerning the Great Proletarian Cultural Revolution," August 8, 1966, https://www.marxists.org/subject/china/peking-review/1966/PR1966-33g.htm.

11. Liu Shaoqi was eventually imprisoned in 1967 and officially expelled from the party in October 1968. He died in prison sometime in 1969.

12. Yiching Wu, "The Other Cultural Revolution: Politics and the Practice of Class in the Chinese Cultural Revolution, 1966–1969" (dissertation, University of Chicago, 2007), 209.

13. Livio Maitan, *Party, Army, and Masses in China: A Marxist Interpretation of the Cultural Revolution and Its Aftermath* (Atlantic Highlands, NJ: Humanities Press, 1976), 110.

14. Paul Bailey, *Women and Gender in Twentieth-Century China* (New York: Palgrave Macmillan, 2012), 124–25. For a general overview of gender in the CR, see ibid., chap. 7; Phyllis Andors, *The Unfinished Liberation of Chinese Women: 1949–1980* (Bloomington: Indiana University Press, 1983), chap. 5; and Kay Ann Johnson, *Women, the Family, and Peasant Revolution in China* (Chicago: Chicago University Press, 1983), chap. 12.

15. Andreas, *Rise of the Red Engineers*, 97.

16. Wu, "The Other Cultural Revolution," 233–39.

17. Ibid., 242.

18. Andreas, *Rise of the Red Engineers*, 108–13.

19. See Dong Guoqiang and Andrew Walder, "Factions in a Bureaucratic Setting: The Origins of Cultural Revolution Conflict in Nanjing," *China Journal* 65 (2011): 1–25; and Guoqiang and Walder, "From Truce to Dictatorship: Creating a Revolutionary Committee in Jiangsu," *China Journal* 68 (2012): 1–32.

20. Elizabeth Perry and Li Xun, *Proletarian Power: Shanghai in the Cultural Revolution* (Boulder: Westview Press, 1997), 33–34.

21. Ibid., 32–35.

22. Ibid., 38.

23. Ibid., 77.

24. Ibid., 87–88.

25. Ibid., 97–99.

26. Ibid., 109–11.

27. Maitan, *Party, Army, and Masses*, 122–26.

28. Perry and Xun, *Proletarian Power*, 150.

29. For a full list of strikes and power seizures in this period, see Maitan, *Party, Army, and Masses*, 126, 162.

30. Roderick MacFarquhar and Michael Schoenhals, *Mao's Last Revolution* (Cambridge, MA: Harvard University Press, 2006), 168.

31. See "On the Revolutionary 'Three-in-One' Combination," *Red Flag* 5, 1967.

32. Dong Guoqiang and Andrew Walder, "Nanjing's Failed 'January Revolution' of 1967: The Inner Politics of a Provincial Power Seizure," *China Quarterly* 203 (2010): 681.

33. Elizabeth Perry and Li Xun, *Proletarian Power: Shanghai in the Cultural Revolution* (Boulder, CO: Westview Press: 1997), 151–52.

34. Ibid., 111.

35. Ibid., 116.

36. Andreas, *Rise of the Red Engineers*, 121–24.

37. Perry and Xun, *Proletarian Power*, 136–38.

38. Ibid., 119.

39. Ibid., 141.

40. Wu, "The Other Cultural Revolution," 262–63.

41. Ibid., 271.

42. For a general overview of this period, see Wu, "The Other Cultural Revolution," chap. 5.

43. Shaoguang Wang, "'New Trends of Thought' on the Cultural Revolution," *Journal of Contemporary China* 21, no. 8 (1999): 203.

44. Jonathan Unger, "Whither China? Yang Xiguang, Red Capitalists, and the Social Turmoil of the Cultural Revolution," *Modern China* 17, no. 1 (1991): 19–22.

45. The Chinese rebels would receive a reply eight months later on May 17, 1968, when students occupying the Sorbonne University in Paris telegrammed the CCP Politburo: "SHAKE IN YOUR SHOES BUREAU-CRATS STOP THE INTERNATIONAL POWER OF THE WORKERS COUNCILS WILL SOON WIPE YOU OUT STOP HUMANITY WON'T BE HAPPY TILL THE LAST BUREAUCRAT IS HUNG WITH THE GUTS OF THE LAST CAPI-TALIST STOP LONG LIVE FACTORY OCCUPATIONS STOP LONG LIVE THE GREAT CHINESE PROLETARIAN REVOLUTION OF 1927 BETRAYED BY THE STALINIST BUREAUCRATS STOP LONG LIVE THE PROLETARIANS OF CANTON AND ELSEWHERE WHO HAVE TAKEN UP ARMS AGAINST THE SO-CALLED PEOPLE'S ARMY STOP LONG LIVE THE CHINESE WORKERS AND STUDENTS WHO HAVE ATTACKED THE SO-CALLED CUL-TURAL REVOLUTION AND THE MAOIST BUREAUCRATIC ORDER STOP LONG LIVE REVOLUTIONARY MARXISM STOP DOWN WITH THE STATE STOP OCCUPATION COMMITTEE OF THE PEOPLE'S FREE SORBONNE." See http://www.cddc.vt.edu/sionline/si/telegrams.html.

46. Roderick MacFarquhar and Michael Schoenhals, *Mao's Last Revolution* (Cambridge, MA: Harvard University Press, 2006), 199.

47. Yiching Wu, *The Cultural Revolution at the Margins: Chinese Socialism in Crisis* (Cambridge, MA: Harvard University Press, 2014), 283n54.

48. Wu, "The Other Cultural Revolution," 279.

49. Ibid., 297.

50. Wang, "'New Trends of Thought,'" 205.

51. For the full text of *Whither China?*, see The 70s Collective, eds., *China: The Revolution Is Dead, Long Live the Revolution!* (Montreal: Black Rose Books, 1977).

52. Wu, "The Other Cultural Revolution," 293–95.

53. Wang, "'New Trends of Thought,'" 208.

54. Wu, "The Other Cultural Revolution," 315–17.

55. Unger, "Whither China?"

56. Wu, "The Other Cultural Revolution," 318.

57. Wang, "'New Trends of Thought,'" 210–12.

58. Andreas, *Rise of the Red Engineers*, 138–40.

59. Crucially, Marx's account of "lower communism" in the *Critique of the Gotha Program* assumes workers will have stopped alienating their products to employers, distributing commodities through markets, and receiving wages in money form. Instead Marx anticipates that they will be able to freely take goods from large collective distribution centers based on a system of labor-time accounting, and that the correspondence between labor-time and consumption will gradually erode as productive forces increase and material plenty develops. Even this conception of a "lower" stage of communism is disputed by anti-state communists, considering the high level of productive forces attained by contemporary capitalism. See "Two Texts on Communisation" on Internationalist-Perspective.org.

60. Raymond Lotta, *Maoist Economics and the Revolutionary Road to Communism: The Shanghai Textbook* (New York: Banner Press, 1994), 24.

61. Ibid., 80.

62. Ibid., 24–25.

63. Ibid., 7.

64. Ibid., 26.

65. Ibid., 62.

66. Ibid., 44–45.

67. Ibid., 63.

68. Ibid., 65–66.

69. Ibid., 109–10.

70. Ibid., 111.

71. Ibid., 145.

72. Ibid., 145.

73. Ibid., 106.

74. Ibid., 108.

75. Ibid., 114.

76. Ibid., 198.

77. The details of the "Lin Piao affair" remain obscure even among China scholars. See Frederick Teiwes and Warren Sun, *The Tragedy of Lin Biao: Riding the Tiger during the Cultural Revolution, 1966–1971* (Honolulu: University of Hawaii Press, 1996).

78. See Perry and Xun, *Proletarian Power*, chap. 6.

79. Yiching Wu, *The Cultural Revolution at the Margins: Chinese Socialism in Crisis* (Cambridge, MA: Harvard University Press, 2014), 25.

80. Charles Bettelheim, *Cultural Revolution and Industrial Organization in China* (New York: Monthly Review Press, 1974), 39–40.

81. Ibid., 22.

82. Ibid., 43.

83. Maitan, *Party, Army, and Masses*, 264–65.

84. Jackie Sheehan, *Chinese Workers: A New History* (New York: Routledge, 1998), 140.

85. See James Tsao, *China's Development Strategies and Foreign Trade* (Lexington: Lexington Books, 1987), 86–98.

86. For an account of the wildcat strikes and protests that took place in this period, see Sheehan, *Chinese Workers*, chap. 5.

87. See Li et al., eds., *On Socialist Democracy and the Chinese Legal System: The Li Yizhe Debates* (Armonk, NY: M.E. Sharpe: 1985).

88. Frederick Teiwes and Warren Sun, *End of the Maoist Era: Chinese Politics during the Twilight of the Cultural Revolution, 1972–76* (New York: Routledge, 2014), 472–75.

89. See Sheehan, *Chinese Workers*, chap. 5.

V. Conclusions

1. For a good overview of these theories, see Marcel van der Linden, *Western Marxism and the Soviet Union: A Survey of Critical Theories and Debates since 1917* (Boston: Brill, 2007).

2. For a similar evaluation of the USSR, see Paresh Chattopadhyay, *The Marxian Concept of Capital and the Soviet Experience* (Westport, CT: Praeger, 1994), 50.

3. Ibid., chap. 1.

4. Karl Marx, *Capital*, vol. 3 (New York: International Publishers, 1984), 436–37.

5. Ibid., 436.

6. See discussion in Chattopadhyay, *The Marxian Concept of Capital*, 26–27.

7. Christopher Howe, *China's Economy: A Basic Guide* (New York: Basic Books, 1978), 42–45.

8. The inability of the Chinese economy under Mao to achieve leaps in productivity is apparent when one compares the sluggish GDP growth of the Maoist era (around 2.2 percent annually) to the exponential trends that followed Deng's reforms in the late 1970s.

9. A. Doak Barnett, *Cadres, Bureaucracy and Political Power in Communist China* (New York: Columbia University Press, 1967), 38–47. See also Franz Schurmann, *Ideology and Organization in Communist China* (Berkeley: University of California Press, 1970), chaps. 2–4.

10. Howe, *China's Economy*, 47–49.

11. Ibid., 180–84.

12. Martin King Whyte and William L. Parish, *Urban Life in Contemporary China* (Chicago: University of Chicago Press, 1984), 86.

13. Ibid., 150–57.

14. Ibid., 42.

15. Ibid., 51–56.

16. Nai-Ruenn Chen and Walter Galenson, *The Chinese Economy Under Communism* (Chicago: Aldine, 1969), 195–97.

17. Howe, *China's Economy*, 19.

18. Mark Selden, *The Political Economy of Chinese Development* (Armonk, NY: M.E. Sharpe, 1993), 175.

19. For the commodity composition of Chinese imports and exports in the Maoist period, see James Tsao, *China's Development Strategies and Foreign Trade* (Lexington: Lexington Books, 1987), 168–71; Chen and Galenson, *The Chinese Economy*, 204–5; and Howe, *China's Economy*, 151.

20. Tsao, *China's Development Strategies*, 83.

21. Ibid., chap. 5.

22. This is true even in the Soviet case, in which commodities sold to China generally matched prices on the world market. See William Kirby, "China's Internationalization in the Early People's Republic," in *The History of the PRC (1949–1976)*, ed. Julia Strauss (Cambridge: Cambridge University Press, 2007), 31.

23. These numbers are based on a comparison of state budget revenues tallied in Chen and Galenson, *The Chinese Economy*, 155, and China's balance of trade, tallied in Tsao, *China's Development Strategies*, 156–57. I gathered the dollar value of Chinese exports from Tsao, converted them using the exchange rate corresponding to that year, and compared this amount with the total state revenue for the corresponding years in Chen and Galenson. My estimate will be slightly skewed due to the fact that the first figures are measured in 1957 and 1959 yuan, and the latter are measured in 1969 yuan. Yet because the yuan's value was generally stable over this period, and was devalued if it changed at all, this discrepancy likely has little impact. At worst it would *underestimate* the ratio of export values to budgetary revenues, since the 1969 figures are in the denominator of the ratio in question.

24. See parts I to IV of Aufheben's "What Was the USSR?," published in series in *Aufheben* 6 (1997) through *Aufheben* 9 (2000), https://libcom. org/library/what-was-ussr-aufheben.

25. See Howe, *China's Economy*, 146–47. In 1974 Chinese enterprises were finally forced to accept lower prices from international buyers at the massive Canton Fair, due to growing dissatisfaction among buyers over the inability of Chinese firms to fulfill contracts reliably.

26. For a discussion of this trend in the USSR, see Chattopadhyay, *The Marxian Concept of Capital*, chaps. 4–5.

27. See Max Elbaum, *Revolution in the Air: Sixties Radicals Turn to Lenin, Mao and Che* (New York: Verso, 2006).

28. See "Long Live Marxism-Leninism-Maoism!," *A World to Win* 20 (1995), http://www.bannedthought.net/International/RIM/AWTW/1995-20/ ll_mlm_20_eng.htm.

29. This vacillation between reductive materialism and idealism was noted by C.L.R. James, Raya Dunayevskaya, and Grace Lee Boggs in 1950: "Stalinism, the ideology of state-capitalism, is the reinstatement of uncritical materialism and uncritical idealism. The materialism is in the accumulation theory. . . . The idealism is in the theory of the party." See C.L.R. James, *State Capitalism and World Revolution* (Oakland: PM Press, 2013), 102.

30. The Western Marxist tradition offers many theorists to draw upon here, including György Lukács, Karl Korsch, Antonio Gramsci, C.L.R. James, Raymond Williams, Stuart Hall, and possibly Pierre Bourdieu.

31. See Newton's speech on the women's liberation and gay liberation movements, in David Hilliard and Kathleen Cleaver, *The Huey P. Newton Reader* (New York: Seven Stories, 2002), 157–60.

32. See Chaitanya Mishra, "The Maoist Crossroads in Nepal: 'Postponing' New Democracy or Sensing Limits of Agency?" Chr. Michelsen Institute, 2014, http://www.cmi.no/file/2570-.pdf. See also Red Marriott, "Nepal: Victory Turns Sour," 2009, https://libcom.org/news/nepal-victory-turns-sour-22012009, and Red Marriott, "Nepalese Maoists Restate Intention to Ban Strikes and Other News," 2009, https://libcom.org/news/nepal-maoists-restate-intention-ban-strikes-other-news-10042009.

■ ABOUT ELLIOTT LIU

Elliott Liu is a political organizer in New York City. He works with the group Take Back the Bronx and the Bronx Social Center.

ABOUT PM PRESS

PM Press was founded at the end of 2007 by a small collection of folks with decades of publishing, media, and organizing experience. PM Press co-conspirators have published and distributed hundreds of books, pamphlets, CDs, and DVDs. Members of PM have founded enduring book fairs, spearheaded victorious tenant organizing campaigns, and worked closely with bookstores, academic conferences, and even rock bands to deliver political and challenging ideas to all walks of life. We're old enough to know what we're doing and young enough to know what's at stake.

We seek to create radical and stimulating fiction and non-fiction books, pamphlets, T-shirts, visual and audio materials to entertain, educate, and inspire you. We aim to distribute these through every available channel with every available technology—whether that means you are seeing anarchist classics at our bookfair stalls; reading our latest vegan cookbook at the café; downloading geeky fiction e-books; or digging new music and timely videos from our website.

PM Press is always on the lookout for talented and skilled volunteers, artists, activists, and writers to work with. If you have a great idea for a project or can contribute in some way, please get in touch.

PM Press
PO Box 23912
Oakland, CA 94623
www.pmpress.org

FRIENDS OF PM PRESS

These are indisputably momentous times—the financial system is melting down globally and the Empire is stumbling. Now more than ever there is a vital need for radical ideas.

In the years since its founding—and on a mere shoestring—PM Press has risen to the formidable challenge of publishing and distributing knowledge and entertainment for the struggles ahead. With hundreds of releases to date, we have published an impressive and stimulating array of literature, art, music, politics, and culture. Using every available medium, we've succeeded in connecting those hungry for ideas and information to those putting them into practice.

Friends of PM allows you to directly help impact, amplify, and revitalize the discourse and actions of radical writers, filmmakers, and artists. It provides us with a stable foundation from which we can build upon our early successes and provides a much-needed subsidy for the materials that can't necessarily pay their own way. You can help make that happen—and receive every new title automatically delivered to your door once a month—by joining as a Friend of PM Press. And, we'll throw in a free T-shirt when you sign up.

Here are your options (all include a 50% discount on all webstore purchases):
- **$30 a month** Get all books and pamphlets
- **$40 a month** Get all PM Press releases (including CDs and DVDs)
- **$100 a month** Everything plus PM merchandise and free downloads

For those who can't afford $30 or more a month, we're introducing **Sustainer Rates** at $15, $10 and $5. Sustainers get a free PM Press T-shirt and a 50% discount on all purchases from our website.

Your Visa or Mastercard will be billed once a month, until you tell us to stop. Or until our efforts succeed in bringing the revolution around. Or the financial meltdown of Capital makes plastic redundant. Whichever comes first.